# Legislative Television as Political Advertising

# Legislative Television as Political Advertising

*

## A Public Choice Approach

*by Franklin G. Mixon, Jr. and Kamal P. Upadhyaya*

iUniverse, Inc.
New York Lincoln Shanghai

# Legislative Television as Political Advertising
## A Public Choice Approach

iUniverse, Inc.

For information address:
iUniverse, Inc.
2021 Pine Lake Road, Suite 100
Lincoln, NE 68512
www.iuniverse.com

ISBN: 0-595-27086-7

Printed in the United States of America

# Contents

# List of Tables

# *About the Book*

Using theoretical and statistical models from recent research, along with several new empirical models and results, this book examines the impact of legislative television on the political process in the United States. Against a theoretical framework wherein political services are considered to have search/experience characteristics, we examine the relationship between political-economic variables and the tendency to adopt/support live television in the U.S. Congress, the impact of television on the length of U.S. House and Senate sessions, the use of parliamentary procedures in the presence (absence) of television cameras, and the role that legislative television has played in improving incumbents' success rates in primary/general federal elections. Where possible, the economic costs to taxpayers of legislators' use of television cameras, in order to enhance their re-election prospects, are also considered. This work should serve as a useful catalogue of current and prior research on the public choice aspects of legislative t.v., as well as a starting point for future research in this area.

# *Preface*

This book is the culmination of a five-year period of concentrated research effort in one area of public choice economics. It has been a fulfilling process, and one that has produced a volume of work that neither of us could have predicted when we initiated this research agenda. As with any significant research effort, a tremendous amount of support was provided to us in this endeavor. First and foremost we thank Troy Gibson and David Hobson, valuable co-authors on many of the research projects detailed in the following pages. Their hard work and dedication, at times in their careers when they were engaged in numerous other academic pursuits, has meant so much to both of us. Len Treviño, Taisa Minto, Ashley Rice and Matthew Tyrone, co-authors of ongoing legislative television projects, have also contributed valuable insights and energy toward promoting and pushing forward this research agenda.

Our previous work has been markedly improved by numerous outside readers. Prominent among these is Mark Crain. He has graciously donated his expertise to us in this and other areas over the past several years. His mentoring is truly appreciated. Numerous other scholars have contributed their time and suggestions to help us carry out our work on legislative television. This list includes Scott Ainsworth, Jürgen Backhaus, Badi Baltagi, Alok Bohara, Steve Caudill, Rohan Christie-David, Shiferaw Gurmu, Peter Kennedy, Steven Levitt, John Lott, Charles Sawyer, Pravin Trivedi, and James Wilkinson. Special thanks goes to John Jackson and Tom Lindley for directing us toward many of the statistical decomposition tests that have become a hallmark of our work in this area. Much of what we know about advertising as information is attributed to the teaching of Richard Ault, Bob Ekelund, David Laband, and the late David Saurman. We owe a great debt to them, and again to Mark Crain and Brian Goff for writing so clearly about this subject.

We are extremely grateful to the University Research Council for supporting our efforts in the Summer of 2000, and to the Business Advisory Council for assisting us financially on numerous occasions since that time. Much of our success is attributable to both of these groups. Lastly, we would like to thank many of our graduate assistants and administrative support staff who have assisted us along the way, and Jay Morris (U.S. House Clerk's office) and Jennifer Manning (Congressional Research Service) for providing us with one-minute speeches data.

Franklin G. Mixon, Jr.
Kamal P. Upadhyaya

January 2003

# 1

# *"Lights…Camera…Action!":*
# *Political Information*
# *Technology's Past and Present*

*"Television is the electronic Acropolis. It has enlarged the audience that can observe and listen to legislators at work. What comes with the expanded audience of the electronic Acropolis are new opportunities for control. Unfortunately, not all of the opportunities are positive from the standpoint of protecting individual liberty. New telecommunications technologies also create new opportunities for manipulation and political abuse." (Crain and Goff, 1988: 2)*

## 1.1 Introduction

"Lights…Camera…Action!" That television has changed the nature of politics is almost without question. Television viewers of the 1960 Presidential debate between Richard Nixon and John Kennedy were, according to surveys, taken aback by Nixon's aged and sallow appearance. On the other hand, they were simultaneously pleased with Kennedy's youthful, robust stature, and signified to pollsters that Kennedy had won the debate. Professional political analysts have since pointed out that much of the perception was due to each candidate's choice of attire. Where Nixon had chosen to wear a light grey suit, Kennedy donned a dark blue suit. On the black-and-white television screen, Nixon's attire blended with the grey background, while Kennedy cast an imposing figure for television audiences. Although television viewers who were polled believed Kennedy had won, most radio listeners—who did not have access to first-hand information on each candidate's physical appearance—believed Nixon had "out-debated" Kennedy (Mixon, 2001). Clearly television had a substantial impact on voters' perceptions, and post-1960 politics in America promised to become significantly different than in earlier periods.

Americans have been watching their federal legislators "at work" via the C-SPAN organization for almost 25 years. The organization uses an annual operating budget of about $36 million and almost 300 employees to offer (1) the C-SPAN network, dedicated to providing gavel-to-gavel coverage of U.S. House proceedings, (2) the C-SPAN2 network, dedicated to providing gavel-to-gavel coverage of U.S. Senate proceedings, and (3) the C-SPAN3 network, which covers public policy forums and special events related to government and politics. These three networks began offering programming in 1979, 1986, and 2001, respectively.

Much like network television entertainment, C-SPAN's programming is run by a private entity (though, in this instance, a non-profit), in this case created through licensing fees, paid by America's cable television (hereafter CATV) systems, rather than advertising revenues paid by businesses. In it's own words, C-SPAN is a "public service" organization dedicated to providing "unedited...balanced views of government, public policy forums..." and elected officials' political activities. In this way, and unlike network television entertainment, C-SPAN's programming is (ostensibly) *un*scripted.

According to a December 2000 survey, 28.5 million people tune into C-SPAN's public affairs programming each week. Those considering themselves to be regular viewers reported an average weekly commitment to C-SPAN's programs of 12 hours. The network's live discussion programs receive a total of 25,000 viewer phone calls each year. Lastly, C-SPAN currently ranks eighth in CATV distribution and is accessible to about 85 million homes.[1] Taken alone, these numbers are staggering. Put into a broader context, they are even more amazing.

For instance, NBC's award-winning television drama about the presidency and national politics, *The West Wing*, garners about 17 million weekly viewers. A popular CATV news network, MSNBC, ranks 34th in cable distribution. And, the music television network MTV is accessible to just over 83 million households via cable.

## 1.2 Legislative Television: A Look Back

Legislative television in the U.S. is not limited to the 25 year-old federal experiment. As Crain and Goff (1988: 15) indicate, televised coverage of state legislatures began several years before the U.S. House opened its doors to C-SPAN's cameras. For instance, Georgia initiated daily legislative television coverage in 1970, and by 1975 almost half of the state legislatures had some form of daily television coverage. Internationally, by the 1980s more than twenty national legislatures permitted television coverage, with many countries beginning their coverage during the early days of television in the 1940s and 1950s (Crain and Goff, 1988: 15). According to Crain and Goff,

> "Once adopted, no national legislature has eliminated television coverage. Several countries, such as Canada, Japan, and the United States televise all or almost all of the official debate. Other national assemblies televise only major debates and debates about the future of government. The French National Assembly is an example of this type of coverage. In many respects the U.S. Congress has lagged behind the other democratic countries with regard to television coverage of the legislative process." (Crain and Goff, 1988: 15-16)

## 1.3 Legislative Television and the Public Choice Approach: A Look Ahead

As the epigraph to this chapter points out, legislative television has been a revolutionary technological innovation, impacting the way we gather political information and reducing the cost of electoral participation. Since Anthony Downs' (1957) work, it has been accepted in public choice theory that if the voter does not pursue politics as a hobby, he or she will be badly informed. This is so because the expected marginal benefit of *this* election outcome or *that* election outcome—which is based upon the likelihood that one's individual vote will determine the election's winner—is very low (or perhaps zero) for a particular voter (see Shachar and Nalebuff, 1999), while the marginal costs associated with political information-gathering and voting (i.e., time/resources spent gathering information about candidates' previous voting records, ideologies and political platforms) can be quite high. The notion that one is badly informed when casting votes in an election, assuming he or she finds it rational to participate at all, is often referred to in the economics literature as *rational ignorance* (see Holcombe, 1996: 170-171).[2]

During the latter half of the twentieth century, however, "information technology has dramatically changed the costs of operating the democratic process in the U.S. (Crain and Goff, 1988: 3)." As in Crain and Goff (1988: 3), we also recognize that "innovations in telecommunications have caused changes in the behavior of voters and legislators." Also as in Crain and Goff (1988), our book will take a look at how legislative television "matters." Following their earlier template, our work will provide updated explorations of the effects of televising legislatures on the length of legislative sessions and the electoral success of incumbent politicians—both of which are impacted by legislator "manipulation" of the sort implied in the epigraph above. We will also synthesize recent work that examines the impact of legislative television in these areas, as well as research on the determinants of the adoption of television and the relationship between television and legislators' use of various parliamentary procedures, such as filibustering and one-minute speeches. Our work follows the Crain-Goff model by establishing the economics of information (Stigler, 1961) and the advertising of goods/services based upon goods-buyer characteristics (Nelson, 1970 and 1974) as the foundation for analysis. Some of what we present is a review of recent research in the field, while much of what fills the subsequent pages is new empirical evidence. Unlike Crain and Goff (1988), however, our work will rely primarily upon empirical observation of the U.S. Congress, rather than state level legislatures. In doing so, our book not only provides a much needed update of Crain and Goff (1988), it also serves as a companion to their earlier work.

## Notes to Chapter 1

1. These and other comparison statistics about C-SPAN are available on the organization's web site at **www.cspan.org.**

2. Boudreaux (1996:117-118) offers a compelling argument in this tradition by asserting that the typical national election involves perhaps thousands of highly aggregated issues—from abortion to school choice to government provision of medical services to farm subsidies to child-welfare policies to tax rates. The fact that each voter has, during a six-year span, a maximum of nine ballots to cast in four national elections suggests that political decisions by voters—as opposed to market decisions by consumers—are *un*informed, and cluttered with "romance pollution" (see also Brennan and Lomasky, 1993). As such, and unlike Wittman's (1995) construct wherein political and market decisions entail similar information components, political decisions are not likely to promote policies with efficient outcomes.

## Chapter 1 References

Boudreaux, D.J. (1996) "Was your high school civics teacher right after all?" *The Independent Review* 1: 111-128.

Brennan, G. and L. Lomasky (1993) *Democracy and decision*, New York, NY: Cambridge University Press.

Crain, W.M. and B.L. Goff (1988) *Televised legislatures: Political information technology and public choice*, Boston, MA: Kluwer Academic Publishers.

cspan.org (2002), Internet web site for the C-SPAN organization.

Downs, A. (1957) *An economic theory of democracy*, New York, NY: Harper & Row Publishers.

Holcombe, R.G. (1996) *Public finance: Government revenues and expenditures in the United States economy*, St. Paul, MN: West Publishing Company.

Mixon, F.G., Jr. (2001) "A discrete-time hazard model of the adoption of legislative television: Evidence from the U.S. Congress, 1961-1986," *Applied Economics* 33: 1,881-1,887.

Nelson, P. (1970) "Information and consumer behavior," *Journal of Political Economy* 77: 311-329.

Nelson, P. "Advertising and information," *Journal of Political Economy* 81: 729-754.

Shachar, R. and B. Nalebuff (1999) "Follow the leader: Theory and evidence on political participation," *American Economic Review* 89: 525-547.

Stigler, G.J. (1961) "The economics of information," *Journal of Political Economy* 68: 213-225.

Wittman, D. (1995) *The myth of democratic failure*, Chicago, IL: University of Chicago Press.

# 2

# *Product Classification and Advertising Qua Information*

*"…you're not anybody in America unless you're on TV…what's the point of doing anything worthwhile if nobody's watching?"*

—Actress Nicole Kidman as Suzanne Stone in the Motion
Picture *To Die For* (1995)

## 2.1 Introduction

The generalized role of advertising in market functioning is now well known. Advertising signals are "technological devices" that reduce the full cost (money plus information plus time) of exchange (Ekelund, Mixon and Ressler, 1995; Mixon 1995). In full equilibrium, suppliers of goods and services provide an "optimal," or utility-and-profit-maximizing, quantity of information or signals to consumers. This information, as Ehrlich and Fisher (1982) have shown, is a derived demand constituting one part of the general equilibrium process by which full price to consumers is minimized and profits to producers are maximized (Ekelund et al., 1995). Suppliers provide a joint product along with goods and services. That product—advertising and all forms of information, such as personal selling or quality signaling—is demanded by consumers to reduce search and other information costs.

## 2.2 Product Classifications and the Provision of Legislative Services

Obviously, the quantity, quality and form of advertising and information provision are functions of buyer *and* goods characteristics, in addition to relative prices (Ekelund et al. 1995). Also, the durability in time and space of the information conveyed is important (Laband, 1989). Nelson (1970 and 1974) suggested an analytical classification of goods with *search* and *experience* characteristics. *Search goods* are those for which quality can be judged by consumers prior to purchase. Stigler (1961) modeled the determinants of a search for the lowest price (by consumers) in reference to a search good (Crain and Goff, 1988: 8).[1] Nelson defined *experience goods* as those for which consumers are unable to judge quality prior to purchase. Darby and Karni (1973) argued, moreover, that some goods were of the *credence* type, the qualities of which cannot be determined even after purchase (e.g., medical surgery, some auto repairs).[2] Most researchers have since argued, however, that search, experience and credence characteristics are components of goods, so that some goods may contain elements of each characteristic.[3]

Demanders of all types of goods will attempt to minimize the information and time costs of exchange, as Stigler (1961) argued in his initial contribution to the transaction costs literature. Consumers will search or sample for prices of goods and services up to the point where the marginal benefit of search equals the marginal cost of search. In his model, the marginal cost of search is a function of the consumer's time cost, as proxied by forgone wages during the search effort, and the (expected) marginal benefit of search is a function of the likelihood that further search would yield a lower price for the consumer. As Stigler (1961) suggests, the marginal benefit of search declines because the probability of locating lower prices decreases with search effort. Advertising (of price) provides the consumer additional information prior to search. Other things being equal, the greater an individual's stock of relevant information concerning a product or service prior to search, the less effort that individual will devote to search for additional information. In this way, and as noted above, advertising reduces the full cost of exchange (money plus goods plus time) to consumers.

Nelson (1970 and 1974) refined Stigler's (1961) original model by indicating that the quantity and/or quality of advertising is not only a function of consumer search costs, but also dependent on the type of good. Given the higher cost of quality verification for experience goods, advertisements for them will contain *indirect* cues of product quality, such as the experience and reputation of the seller.[4] These indirect cues are verifiable at low cost, and the buyer can make inferences about product quality using these. Theoretical research (see Emons, 2001) has extended Nelson's construct, and empirical tests have verified his hypothesis concerning the *indirect* forms of advertising for experience (and credence) goods (see Laband, 1986; Ekelund, Mixon and Ressler, 1995; Mixon, 1995).[5]

The economics of information and the theory of product advertising are easily adaptable to analyzing political transactions and the provision of legislative services by legislators. According to Crain and Goff (1988: 7):

> "When voters vote, their choices are influenced by what they know about candidates. What is not known is similarly influential. What voters know and do not know depends on how much it costs to become informed politically. Individuals take into consideration the costs of political information in political transactions, just as in the market."

Crain and Goff (1988) state that one branch of analysis simply applies the product advertising models described above to political advertising (Nelson, 1976; Telser, 1976; Ferguson, 1976). Nelson holds that political advertisements contain primarily direct information (i.e., information about specific characteristics of candidates). According to Crain and Goff (1988: 11):[6]

"Candidates' service records are available. Voters can compare the actual records with the promises of candidates. Political advertisements will contain truthful statements because voters can easily detect dissonance between the advertised message and past performance. This implies that legislative services are search goods. Voters compare detailed characteristics of candidates before voting."

As Crain and Goff point out, both Telser (1976) and Ferguson (1976) disagree. Telser views political services as experience goods because it "is difficult for voters to draw inferences about the future behavior of candidates (Crain and Goff, 1988: 11)." Additionally, voters have little incentive to compare a candidate's *advertised qualities* with his or her *actual qualities*, because the benefits of doing so to any single voter are small, while the costs of gathering political information can be substantial (Crain and Goff, 1988).[7] Information acquisition costs, and thus rational ignorance, suggest that legislative services are similar to experience goods.

## 2.3 Media Coverage of State and Federal Legislative Services: Which Gets More?

In either case above, whether legislative services are viewed as primarily search goods or primarily experience goods, any technological advancement that changes the costs of information gathering by voters will alter the nature of political services (Crain and Goff, 1988). Because televising legislative proceedings lowers the costs of evaluating a politician's *advertised qualities* against his or her *actual qualities*, legislative services will encompass more search goods characteristics. It is within this framework that we analyze the impact of television on the legislative process. However, in doing so we argue that there are differences between state-level legislative services, which were the primary focus of Crain and Goff (1988), and federal legislative services (i.e., the U.S. Congress), the primary focus of this book. Voting records for members of the U.S. Congress have always been more accessible than those at the state level, due in large part to coverage by nationally circulated periodicals, widely circulated newspapers, and cable television networks. Coverage in these media is augmented further by Washington D.C.-based print media specializing in federal political matters. All of these sources, through which federal politics is more accessible to citizens-voters, are listed in Table 2.1.

### Table 2.1 Print/Video Media Coverage of National Politics *

Nationally Circulated Periodicals: *Time, Newsweek,* and *U.S. News & World Report*

Widely Circulated Newspapers: *Chicago Tribune, Los Angeles Times, New York Times, Wall Street Journal, Washington Post,* and *Washington Times*

Cable TV Networks: CNBC, CNN, Fox-News, HNN, and MSNBC

Washington, D.C.-based print media: *Congress Daily, The Hill, Roll Call*

---

\*   Sources: Mixon, Hobson and Upadhyaya (2001); Mixon and Upadhyaya (2002).

Federal legislators also have significantly larger operating budgets than their state-level counterparts, and they often use them to provide their voting records and other political information to their constituents. Think tanks and congressional watchdogs, such as the Progressive Policy Institute, The Cato Institute, The Heritage Foundation, Americans for Tax Reform, and the National Taxpayers Union, publish and distribute vote-rating guides on all U.S. Representatives and Senators for practically every broad issue that comes before the U.S. Congress over a two-year period. The advent of the Internet, and web magazines such as *Slate*, has made gathering these types of informational cues easier for voters concerned with federal politics (Mixon et al., 2001).

One other difference between federal and state legislatures concerns the types of voting devices used in the U.S. Congress. Voters cannot determine, through the C-SPAN medium, exactly how a particular legislator voted at the time of a bill's passage or failure. Although the U.S. House uses an electronic device to record votes, only Party totals are displayed on the television screen by C-SPAN cameras (Mixon, et al.,

2001). Similarly, although the U.S. Senate uses a voice roll-call system to record votes, C-SPAN2 almost always tunes out individual votes by playing classical music and displaying only Party totals on the television screen for viewers. On the other hand, the wide variety of techniques used to televise state legislatures permits some voters to record individual votes cast by representatives. Unlike at the federal level, this may be their only source of information. These examples all suggest that federal legislative services have historically been more like search goods than their state level counterparts, and have been affected less in this way (i.e., in terms of providing information on actual votes cast) by television coverage. These considerations across political tiers do not, however, diminish the perennial need for federal politicians to advertise and engage in fundraising to secure and protect their elected positions. The remaining chapters of this book focus on how that advertising effort, and other forms of political behavior, have changed since the adoption of television coverage in the federal legislature.

## 2.4 Concluding Comments

Media coverage of federal legislative services is expansive, ranging from nationally circulated print outlets to cable television news networks. Among the many differences between the federal legislature and its 50 state-level counterparts, is the vast attention (and scrutiny) that the federal legislature receives in the media. One would expect, therefore, that federal legislative services are more like search goods relative to their state-level counterparts, other things constant. We also argue in this chapter that, given the types of voting devices used in the U.S. Congress and the methods used by C-SPAN for covering congressional votes, federal legislative television (i.e., C-SPAN) has done little, at least relative to state-level legislative television, to provide information on actual votes, suggesting that legislative television has not done as much to move federal legislative services closer to the *search goods* pole on the *search-experience* continuum as it perhaps has in the state legislatures.

Given this argument, how has legislative television been viewed, and perhaps used, by U.S. Representative and Senators? After all, a politician must advertise his/her message and engage in fundraising during, and often before, election periods, in order to secure his/her incumbency. As in Crain and Goff (1988), we recognize that innovations in telecommunications have caused changes in the behavior of legislators (and voters) in terms of advertising/campaigning. As we stated above, and as in Crain and Goff (1988), our book will take a look at how legislative television "matters" in this regard. This exploration constitutes the focus of the remaining chapters.

## Notes to Chapter 2

1. Crain and Goff (1988: 8) point out that Stigler and Nelson defined search goods somewhat differently. Our analysis uses Nelson's definitions.

2. The expectation that one will understand quality characteristics over some relevant time period is low for many credence goods. For goods with credence characteristics, as well as those with experience characteristics, the finding of optimal quality and quantity pre- or post-sale is a matter of employing costly resources or of assuming risk. The highest cost may attach to credence goods. As Ekelund et al. (1995: 41) suggest, "We would not argue…that some optimal quality and quantity could (theoretically) *never* be determined by consumers, although pure credence goods, such as religion or voodoo, may be recognized as such."

3. Crain and Goff (1988) make a similar point by arguing that very few goods, including political services, are entirely search or experience. Rather, most goods have characteristics of both types. A continuum exists between the polar cases of search and experience (or credence), and most goods fall somewhere in between (Crain and Goff, 1988:8). Relatedly, Laband (1991) found that price is a reasonable proxy for

search and experience characteristics, although he did not consider credence characteristics. His construct is used/verified in Mixon (1999).

4. Other things being equal, consumers may well demand more information for goods with experience characteristics than they do for goods with credence characteristics, although it appears reasonable to hypothesize that the information content of advertisements for credence goods would appear much the same as that in advertisements for experience goods (Ekelund et al. 1995: 40).

5. Ekelund et al. (1995) and Mixon (1995) use common lists for search, experience, and credence goods and services. Examples of these are (1) photo-finishing, lumber, liquor, and books, and (2) carpet cleaning, travel agents, roofing contractors, and jewelers, and (3) home security systems, palm readers, martial arts lessons, and tax services, respectively.

6. Combined with Wittman's (1995) notion that voters are fully informed, in this view legislative services contain mostly search characteristics.

7. Crain and Goff (1988) point out that Nelson ignores the disincentives facing voters. Nelson suggests that opposing candidates are able to provide information about past performance of their opposition. However, a credibility problem exists when a challenger presents information about his or her opponent. Voters must filter this information and assign some probability to the truthfulness of the message. The incentive problem is only moved back one step (Crain and Goff, 1988: 12).

## Chapter 2 References

Crain, W.M. and B.L. Goff (1988) *Televised legislatures: Political information technology and public choice*, Boston, MA: Kluwer Academic Publishers.

Darby, M.R. and E. Karni (1973) "Free competition and the optimal amount of fraud," *Journal of Law and Economics* 16: 67-88.

Ehrlich, I. and L. Fisher (1982) "The derived demand for advertising," *American Economic Review* 72: 366-388.

Ekelund, R.B., Jr., F.G. Mixon, Jr. and R.W. Ressler (1995) "Advertising and information: An empirical study of search, experience and credence goods," *Journal of Economic Studies* 22: 33-43.

Emons, W. (2001) "Credence goods monopolists," *International Journal of Industrial Organization* 19: 375-389.

Ferguson, J. (1976) "Political information: Comment," *Journal of Law and Economics* 19: 341-346.

Laband, D.N. (1986) "Advertising as information: An empirical note," *Review of Economics and Statistics* 68: 517-521.

Laband, D.N. (1989) "The durability of informational signals and the content of advertising," *Journal of Advertising* 18: 13-18.

Laband, D.N. (1991) "An objective measure of search versus experience goods," *Economic Inquiry* 29: 497-509.

Mixon, F.G., Jr. (1995) "Advertising as information: Further evidence," *Southern Economic Journal* 61: 1,213-1,218.

Mixon, F.G., Jr. (1999) "Customer return policies for experience goods: The impact of product price and consumer search costs on seller-provided informational cues," *Applied Economics* 31: 331-336.

Mixon, F.G., Jr., D.L. Hobson and K.P. Upadhyaya (2001) "Gavel-to-gavel congressional television as political advertising: The impact of C-SPAN on legislative sessions," *Economic Inquiry* 39: 351-364.

Mixon, F.G., Jr. and K.P. Upadhyaya (2002) "Legislative television as an institutional entry barrier: The impact of C-SPAN2 on turnover in the U.S. Senate, 1946-1998," *Public Choice* 112: 433-448.

Nelson, P. (1970) "Information and consumer behavior," *Journal of Political Economy* 77: 311-329.

Nelson, P. (1974) "Advertising and information," *Journal of Political Economy* 81: 729-754.

Nelson, P. (1976) "Political Information," *Journal of Law and Economics* 19: 315-336.

Stigler, G.J. (1961) "The economics of information," *Journal of Political Economy* 68: 213-225.

Telser, L. (1976) "Political information: Comment," *Journal of Law and Economics* 19: 337-340.

Wittman, D. (1995) *The myth of democratic failure*, Chicago, IL: University of Chicago Press.

# 3

# *The Adoption of Legislative Television in the U.S. Congress: A Public Choice Retrospective*

*"The names of Gingrich and Walker became household names due to the C-SPAN coverage of the U.S. House. Before televised sessions they would have been two relatively unknown members of the minority party." (Crain and Goff, 1988: 58)*

## 3.1 Introduction

Despite the fact that surveys report the number of C-SPAN watchers in the millions, very little empirical work exists in the economics literature on its political origins. Crain and Goff (1988) and Mixon (2001) have provided the only extensive studies on the efforts to adopt television in state legislative branches and the U.S. Congress. The latter of these uses data from the U.S. House of Representatives and the U.S. Senate during the 1961-1986 time period to explore the correlates of adoption (and non-adoption) of television (i.e., C-SPAN/C-SPAN2). During the latter part of this time frame, C-SPAN began providing full-time gavel-to-gavel coverage of the U.S. House (1982), and C-SPAN2 began lengthy coverage of U.S. Senate proceedings (1986).

The previous chapter presented a detailed discussion of the primary differences between state-level legislatures and their federal counterpart. The point was made there that federal legislative services have historically been more like *search goods* than state-level services, and that voting mechanisms used in various state legislatures permit, unlike C-SPAN, voters to record the votes cast be their own representatives in the state legislature (Mixon, Hobson and Upadhyaya, 2001). Given the diverse constituencies facing many state legislators, passage of legislative television could be harmful to many incumbents' re-election bids, and thus would result in attempts to prevent its implementation (Crain and Goff, 1988). In this sense, passage of state-level legislative television would, in many cases, change the basic nature of the political services provided by state-level legislatures. Such a change would be represented by a movement toward the *search goods* pole on the goods-characteristics continuum.

As Chapter 2 argued, federal politics have historically been more like *search goods* than their state-level counterparts, and television has done little to change the nature of federal legislative services. In the U.S. Congress, therefore, rules of the House and Senate, such as One Minute Speeches, filibustering, and Special Order Speeches, would allow legislators the opportunity to "grandstand" on popular issues, as a form of political advertising, in front of television cameras. As such, there would not be the more general antipathy toward legislative television in the Congress that exists throughout some of the 50 states.

Within this same construct, however, the presence of entrenched incumbency in the 1970s/1980s U.S. House and Senate would provide resistance to the televising of legislative proceedings there. Risk averse, vote-maximizing senior incumbent Representatives and Senators would likely present significant internal opposition to television due to uncertainty regarding its effects on future vote production (Mixon, 2001: 1,882). However, homogeneity of the population/constituency facing incumbents at the federal level presents an opposing force to the uncertainty (Crain and Goff, 1988). Such force results from some legislators' belief that television could be helpful, other things constant. Both the internal and external factors are important determinants of the adoption of legislative television at the federal level, and they are explored by Mixon (2001). The remaining sections of this chapter detail the construct and findings of the recent study by Mixon.

## 3.2 A Framework for Analyzing the Adoption of Legislative T.V.

A theoretical framework for the television adoption decision in the federal legislature is developed in Mixon (2001) and is based on the lottery adoption model developed by Caudill, Ford, Mixon and Peng (1995). These authors, following the public choice paradigm, view politicians as vote maximizers, where legislative television can be viewed as a means (impediment) to achieving that end. Mixon (2001) assumes that the legislative tendency in either branch of the U.S. Congress toward television adoption is given by an *un*observable variable, $Y^*$. What can be observed is the outcome of a vote to adopt legislative television in either branch, or $Y$. If $Y^* \geq 0$ in a branch of Congress, legislative television is adopted in that branch and $Y=1$. If $Y^*<0$, legislative television fails to get majority support in that branch and is not adopted; in this case, $Y=0$ (Mixon, 2001: 1,882). It is also assumed that a reduced-form model of the legislative tendency toward television adoption in a Congressional branch is given as:

(3.1) $Y_i^* = X_i\beta + \varepsilon_i,$

where $X_i$ is a vector of exogenous variables representing internal and external pressures on the adoption decision, $\beta$ is a vector of parameters to be estimated, and $\varepsilon_i$ is a random error term. If $\varepsilon_i$ is assumed to follow the standard logistic distribution, then the probability of the adoption of legislative television in a given year by a branch of Congress is given by the familiar logit formula (see Kennedy, 1998; Greene, 2003):

(3.2) $P = [\exp(X_i\beta)]/[1 + \exp(X_i\beta)].$

The probability that legislative television is not adopted in a given year by a branch of Congress is $1-P$. Following Mixon (2001: 1,883), at each year in the sample, a branch of the U.S. Congress either adopts legislative television or does not adopt legislative television, with probabilities $P$ and $1-P$, respectively.

The Mixon study uses probabilities like those in equation (3.2) to estimate a discrete-time hazard model of legislative television adoption in the U.S. Congress. According to Mixon (2001: 1,883):

> "What is actually modeled is the timing of the legislative television adoption decision. A branch of the U.S. Congress that adopts legislative television early contributes more information on the determinants of television adoption than the other branch, and a branch adopting television later (or not at all) provides more information about the determinants of non-adoption. Thus, the timing aspect is presented accordingly."

In Mixon's (2001) hazard model, data on independent variables in a given year are used to determine the probability of adoption in that year (see also Caudill et al., 1995).[1] When possible, discrete-time hazard models are estimated by maximum likelihood.[2]

## 3.3 Adoption of Legislative Television in the U.S. Congress: Examining the Crain-Goff and Mixon Analyses

Mixon's (2001) study compiled a pooled data set to examine the legislative television adoption decision in the U.S. Congress. Data were drawn on each congressional branch (cross-section) for the years (time series) 1961-1986 (inclusive). The data set contained a total of 48 observations. Mixon's (2001) dependent variable is ADOPT, a dummy variable equal to one if legislative branch $I$ adopts legislative television in a given year, $t$. ADOPT equals zero until the congressional branch adopts television; when television is adopted, ADOPT equals one. "Beyond the year of adoption, no additional observations from that congressional branch are used (Mixon, 2001: 1,883)." Mixon's

(2001) study models "the year of adoption" in each branch of Congress as the year in which the branch began "extensive" coverage of legislative proceedings.[3] Regarding the year of adoption in each branch, Mixon indicates:

> "As the C-SPAN website points out, C-SPAN began televising U.S. House proceedings in 1979, the year used by Crain and Goff (1986) in their analysis of the effects of legislative television on behavior. This study [Mixon, 2001] chooses 1982 because it was the first year C-SPAN was allowed extended coverage in the U.S. House (16 hours per day). Extensive coverage allows viewers the ability to watch outside of daily work schedules…Extensive Senate coverage began in 1986, so it is included as such in the model. Both time series (House and Senate) begin in 1961…The present study selects 1961 as the starting point because (1) electronic technology had advanced to the point that televised proceedings fell easily within the scope of feasibility, and (2) viewer response to the 1960 Kennedy-Nixon Presidential debate suggested that the impact of television on the political process was nontrivial." (Mixon, 2001: 1,883)

The following list of independent variables was employed by Mixon (2001: 1,883-1,884):

SENATE:     a dummy variable equal to one for Senate observations in the panel data set, and zero otherwise.

CSERV:      the percentage of each congressional branch's roster with 12 or more years of consecutive service in that particular branch.

OBRANCH:    a dummy variable equal to one (for each branch) if the other branch has adopted television at that time, and zero otherwise.

BLK:        the ratio of each legislative branch represented by Black legislators in a given year, and zero otherwise.

PREZ:       a dummy variable equal to one if the majority political party in a legislative branch and the Administration are the same (in a given year), and zero otherwise.

LFPR:       the labor force participation rate in the U.S. each year.

| UNION: | the percentage of the U.S. workforce belonging to labor unions each year. |
| --- | --- |
| VRA82: | a dummy variable equal to one for 1982 and thereafter, and zero otherwise. This variable captures passage of the *Voting Rights Act of 1982.* |
| MAJ: | the ratio of majority party legislators to total legislators in each branch of the U.S. Congress for each year. |

The SENATE variable is included by Mixon to test for any institutional divide on the probability of adoption (Mixon, 2001: 1,883). As Mixon, Hobson and Upadhyaya (2001) suggest, the U.S. Constitution and Senate rules create a more deliberate body in the Senate (relative to the House), and Senators will be expected to act in ways that protect and respect their historical traditions in this regard.

As Crain and Goff (1988) point out, politicians base their support for/opposition to legislative television on how its presence is expected to impact their electoral success. Length of service will determine support or dissent on televised sessions within a legislative chamber. As Mixon indicates:

> "First, 'older legislators, who developed their political skills before television's impact became so large, will use television less effectively than younger legislators (Crain and Goff, 1988: 59).' Second, the seniority system can sometimes 'be bypassed by skilled use of television. Lawmakers who have spent a lifetime in building a reputation will not support a technological move that allows younger lawmakers to gain the same amount of visibility in a fraction of the time (Crain and Goff, 1988: 60).'" (Mixon, 2001: 1,884)

The existence of television in one branch of Congress (OBRANCH) is expected to influence the decision to adopt in the other branch. According to Crain and Goff (1988), televising sessions is one way that members of a legislative chamber can increase their exposure and influence relative to the other chamber (Mixon, 2001: 1,884). If one branch has already adopted, pressure to adopt in the other branch grows, given the exposure disadvantage faced by the non-televised branch.

Congruence between the majority party of a congressional branch and the presidency (PREZ) is also considered in Mixon (2001).

> "When one party controls both a chamber of Congress and the White House, adoption of television is less likely. Crain and Goff (1986) point out that the executive branch has used television coverage to its advantage for a long time. Accordingly, television coverage of legislative sessions is one way Congress can compensate for the visibility advantage of the Presidency. This compensation will, however, be less important when there is political party congruence among the two arms of government." (Mixon, 2001: 1,884)

The variable VRA82 is based on the 1982 amendments to the *Voting Rights Act of 1965*, which allowed for the creation of Congressional districts with "protected class" considerations (i.e., districts where national minorities represent a majority of the electorate). Following Will (1992) and Mixon and Upadhyaya (1997), this legislation created odd-shaped Congressional districts with less demographic/political diversity.

> "As Crain and Goff suggest, 'to the extent that legislators from homogeneous constituencies recognize the benefits of coverage on their vote productions, they have an incentive to vote in favour of televised sessions (1988: 59).' Since *VRA82* created more homogeneous legislative districts, its passage is expected to reduce the risk of lower vote production [one might otherwise associate with]…televising legislative sessions (see Crain and Goff, 1988)." (Mixon, 2001: 1,884-1,885)

Two additional political variables are considered (BLK and MAJ). Because Black legislators usually represent more homogeneous districts (i.e., solidly Democratic areas), Black legislators will view the prospect of legislative television differently than non-blacks (see discussion on

VRA82 above). Additionally, party security, like individual job security, is expected to influence support (dissent) when political parties cannot fully know and anticipate all of television's ramifications. "If political parties, like the individuals who comprise them, are risk averse, then narrow [(wide)] majority margins are likely to lead to non-adoption [(adoption)] (Mixon, 2001: 1,885)." Lastly, the Mixon (2001) study, like that of Crain and Goff (1988), includes two other demographic measures of constituent homogeneity (LFPR and UNION) not discussed in detail here.

To synthesize the conceptual arguments, SENATE, CSERV, and PREZ are all expected to be negatively related to the probability of television adoption (ADOPT) in a particular branch of Congress. OBRANCH, VRA82, BLK, and MAJ are all expected to be positively related to ADOPT. As Mixon (2001: 1,885) points out, estimation of the model by maximum likelihood proved problematic.[4] A linear probability model (LPM) was, therefore, substituted for logit estimation.

Results from Mixon's (2001) analysis are presented in general format, along with those from the 1986 Senate vote on C-SPAN2 in Crain and Goff (1988) for comparison, in Table 3.1.

### Table 3.1 LPM Regression Results on Congressional "Adoption" of Legislative T.V. [*]

|  | Crain-Goff (1988) Study | Mixon (2001) Study |
|---|---|---|
| dependent variable: | dummy variable equal to 1 if a Senator voted "yes" on legislative t.v., and 0 otherwise | dummy variable equal to 1 if a Congressional branch adopts legislative t.v., and zero otherwise |
| sample period: | 1986 | 1961-1986 |
| number of observations: | 100 | 48 |
| Regression Controls: |  |  |

## Table 3.1 LPM Regression Results on Congressional "Adoption" of Legislative T.V. (Continued)[*]

| | *Crain-Goff (1988) Study* | *Mixon (2001) Study* |
|---|---|---|
| Length of service for legislators: | tenure of Senators is negatively and significantly related to the the probability that a Senator votes "yes" for t.v. [YELECT] | tenure of legislators is negatively and significantly related to adoption of t.v. by each Congressional branch [CSERV] |
| Constituent diversity: | more homogeneous constituencies increase the likelihood that a Senator votes "yes" for t.v., though not significantly [DED] | more homogeneous constituencies significantly increase the likelihood that a Congressional branch adopts legislative t.v. [LFPR; UNION; VRA82; BLK] |
| Senator/Party security or risk aversion: | Senators who captured wide margins in last election are significantly more likely to vote "yes" for t.v. [LVOTE]; Senators up for re-election in the year of the t.v. vote are less likely to vote "yes" for t.v., though not significantly [D86] | larger majority Party representation in a Congressional branch is positively related to the probability that the branch adopts t.v., though not significantly [MAJ] |
| Political visibility: | | If one branch has already adopted, the other branch is significantly more likely to adopt [OBRANCH]; if the majority Party in a branch and the sitting President's Party are the same, that branch is significantly less likely to adopt legislative t.v. [PREZ] |

**Table 3.1 LPM Regression Results on Congressional "Adoption" of Legislative T.V. (Continued)***

|  | Crain-Goff (1988) Study | Mixon (2001) Study |
|---|---|---|
| Information demand: | Senators from states with a higher percentage of white collar workers are significantly more likely to vote "yes" for t.v., given that higher income constituents have a greater demand for information [PCTWC] | |
| Range of reported R-squares | 0.249 to 0.253 | 0.08 to 0.35 |

* Note: Abbreviations in brackets in the description of the results represent the variable names used in the respective studies. The Mixon (2001) results come from two separate tables in that study.

Though the dependent variables in Crain and Goff (1988) and Mixon (2001) are different, the idea behind each statistical exploration is generally the same. The two sets of results are remarkably supportive of one another. Among the results in Mixon (2001) mentioned in Table 3.1 above, the presence of television in one branch of Congress exerts pressure on the other branch to adopt (i.e., OBRANCH is positive and significant). As Mixon points out, this is consistent with the view that one branch's relative power within the legislature is a function of the exposure gained by it and the other branch. In response to increased (potential) exposure from television in the other branch, the non-adopter is more likely to opt for television (which the Senate did in 1986). Though not listed in Table 3.1, Mixon's (2001) results also indicate that the more deliberative legislative branch—the U.S. Senate—is less likely than the House (in any year prior to adoption in either branch) to allow its methods of operation to be altered by the possibilities of television, *ceteris paribus*.

As Table 3.1 points out, the tenure of legislators in a legislative body is negatively related to support for legislative television by an individual legislator or by the legislative body as a whole. Variables in both the

Crain and Goff (1988) and Mixon (2001) studies suggest that risk aversion (job security), or one's expectation of the impact legislative television will have on one's future vote production, exhibits pressure on individual Senators or the legislative body as a whole to oppose (support) legislative television. The degree of constituent homogeneity is positively related to support for legislative television by individual Senators and legislative bodies as a whole (see Table 3.1).

Not only are the Crain-Goff (1988) and Mixon (2001) findings generally supportive of one another, recent empirical investigation into the determinants of the 1977 vote to adopt television in the U.S. has yielded some interesting findings (Tyrone et al., 2003). For instance, as in Crain and Goff (1988), Representatives who received larger victory margins in the 1976 general elections were significantly more likely to cast a vote in favor of C-SPAN cameras in 1977, other things constant. Constituent homogeneity (DED) and a greater demand for political information by constituents (PCTWC) are positively related to a Representative's vote on C-SPAN cameras. This finding mirrors that for the 1986 Senate vote in Crain and Goff (1988).

## 3.4 Concluding Comments

Most, if not all, of the variables considered by Crain and Goff (1988) and Mixon (2001) in examining a legislator's or legislature's tendency to support legislative television capture some element of self-interest. "Public choice theorists usually begin with the working behavioral postulate of self-interest. It is natural for the public choice economist to question new institutions in terms of how the self-interests of individuals [i.e., Senators], or groups of individuals [i.e., the U.S. House and/or the U.S. Senate] are affected by them (Crain and Goff, 1988: 2)." That many of the variables in the regressions reviewed in this chapter were significant determinants of the adoption of legislative television supports this simple, but fundamental, assumption in public choice.

# Notes to Chapter 3

1. Mixon (2001) points out that, although hazard models are widely used in economics, discrete-time hazard models are less common. Examples of the latter are provided by Holden, Burkhauser, and Feaster (1988), Myers, Burkhauser, and Holden (1987), Allison (1982), and Caudill et al. (1995).

2. See Caudill et al. (1995) and Mixon (2001) for the various probability expressions related to discrete-time hazard models.

3. There are, of course, alternative methods, such as modeling the year of adoption as the year in which each branch voted (by majority) to allow television coverage. This occurred in 1977 in the U.S. House of Representatives and in 1986 for the Senate. Crain and Goff (1988) model the adoption of television in the Senate by analyzing the determinants of each of the 100 votes (by Senators) on television (C-SPAN2) adoption in 1986. A more recent study by Tyrone, Mixon, Trevino, and Minto (2003) models the adoption of television in the House by analyzing the determinants of each of the 386 votes (by Representatives) on television (C-SPAN) adoption in 1977. As we explain later in this chapter, the discrete-time results in Mixon (2001) support those in Crain and Goff (1988), and are further supported by the recent work of Tyrone et al. (2003).

4. As the statistical literature indicates, estimation of some limited dependent variables models by maximum likelihood is problematic (see Anderson, 1987; Caudill, 1987 and 1988; Oskanen, 1986). Inclusion of observation-specific dummy variables or group dummy variables, in which most or all of the members of the "group members" make the same "choice," leads to such estimation problems. Use of OBRANCH and VRA82 present such a problem in Mixon's analysis. Caudill (1987 and 1988) provides a rationale for the use of linear probability models (LPM) as a substitute for logit or probit in the presence

of such problems. The Crain-Goff (1988) Senate vote model mentioned earlier in the Chapter also makes use of LPM.

# Chapter 3 References

Allison, P.D. (1982) "Discrete-time methods for the analysis of event histories," *Sociological Methodology* 13: 61-98.

Anderson, P.D. (1987) "Prediction tests in limited dependent variable models," *Journal of Econometrics* 34: 253-261.

Caudill, S.B. (1987) "Dichotomous choice models and dummy variables," *The Statistician* 36: 381-383.

Caudill, S.B. (1988) "An advantage of the linear probability model over probit or logit," *Oxford Bulletin of Economics and Statistics* 50: 425-427.

Caudill, S.B., J.M. Ford, F.G. Mixon, Jr. and T.C. Peng (1995) "A discrete-time hazard model of lottery adoption," *Applied Economics* 27: 555-561.

Crain, W.M. and B.L. Goff (1988) *Televised legislatures: Political information technology and public choice*, Boston, MA: Kluwer Academic Publishers.

Greene, W.H. (2003) *Econometric analysis*, Upper Saddle River, NJ: Prentice Hall.

Holden, K.C., R.V. Burkhauser, and D.J. Feaster (1988) "The timing of falls into poverty after retirement and widowhood," *Demography* 25: 405-414.

Kennedy, P. (1998) *A guide to econometrics*, Cambridge, MA: The MIT Press.

Mixon, F.G., Jr. (2001) "A discrete-time hazard model of the adoption of legislative television: Evidence from the U.S. Congress, 1961-1986," *Applied Economics* 33: 1,881-1,887.

Mixon, F.G., Jr., D.L. Hobson and K.P. Upadhyaya (2001) "Gavel-to-gavel congressional television coverage as political advertising: The impact of C-SPAN on legislative sessions," *Economic Inquiry* 39: 351-364.

Mixon, F.G., Jr. and K.P. Upadhyaya (1997) "Gerrymandering and the *Voting Rights Act of 1982*: A public choice analysis of turnover in the U.S. House of Representatives," *Public Choice* 93: 357-371.

Myers, O.A., R.V. Burkhauser, and K.C. Holden (1987) "The transition from wife to widow: The importance of survivor benefits to widows," *Journal of Risk and Insurance* 54: 752-759.

Oskanen, E.H. (1986) "A note on observation-specific dummies and logit analysis," *The Statistician* 35: 413-416.

Tyrone, J.M., F.G., Mixon, Jr., L.J. Trevino, and T.C. Minto (2003) "Politics and the adoption of legislative television: An analysis of the U.S. House vote on C-SPAN," *European Journal of Law and Economics*, forthcoming.

Will, G.F. (1992) *Restoration: Congress, term limits and the recovery of deliberative democracy*, New York, NY: The Free Press.

# 4

# *Has Legislative Television Mattered? New Evidence on U.S. Senate Session Lengths*

*"...politicians often engage in persuasive advertising campaigns to win the production contract from their constituencies... We provide evidence...suggest[ing] that [U.S.] House sessions have become longer as a result of the presence of C-SPAN cameras."* (Mixon, Hobson and Upadhyaya, 2001: 364)

## 4.1 Introduction

This chapter extends, in several areas, the work of Mixon, Hobson and Upadhyaya (2001), that examines the length of U.S. House *and* Senate proceedings over time. First, we concentrate solely on Senate proceedings, and we use annual time series data from 1972-2001. Second, more substantive diagnostic testing of the time series data set is implemented here. Third, and unlike Mixon et al. (2001), this study decomposes the differences in the average lengths of Senate proceedings in the pre- and post-C-SPAN2 eras in order to highlight the effects of C-SPAN2 cameras on Senate proceedings. These differences are also treated as stochastic by performing various significance tests on the decomposition measures. Use of U.S. Senate data is appropriate given that various parliamentary procedures (e.g., filibustering, Morning

Business, Special Order Speeches, etc.) potentially serve Senate incumbents as low-cost advertising through television coverage (see Krehbiel, 1998). Our economic model of Senate session lengths, and the empirical results, are described in the next section of this chapter.

## 4.2 Economic Model and Empirical Results

This chapter presents a model similar to the more parsimonious tests included in Mixon et al. (2001). It is given below:

(4.1) $SESRVOTES_t = a_0 + b_1CSPAN_t + b_2DEM_t + b_3GGDP_t + b_4PREZ_t + u,$

where SESRVOTES is equal to the length of annual U.S. Senate proceedings (in days) divided by the number of recorded votes produced each year in the U.S. Senate (*CQ Almanac*, 1972-2001). This series is measured during the post-war period (i.e., beginning in 1972), and runs through 2001. As in Mixon et al. (2001), we index proceedings time (in days) by a "productivity" measure, namely the number of recorded votes produced in the Senate annually. This construct essentially means that SESRVOTES measures the amount of time (in days) spent per bill or resolution voted on (recorded).[1]

The regressors included:

CSPAN = a dummy variable equal to one for years in which C-SPAN2 covered Senate proceedings, and zero otherwise. Senate coverage began in 1986.

DEM = the proportion of the Senate made up of Democrats each year.

GGDP = federal government expenditures as a percent of GDP each year.

PREZ = a dummy variable equal to 1 for Presidential election years, and zero otherwise.

If the thesis in this book and in Mixon et al. (2001) is correct, the variable C-SPAN will be positively related to SESRVOTES. That is, greater levels of political grandstanding—as a form of low-cost advertising—will be reflected in greater amounts of time spent per recorded vote annually in the U.S. Senate.[2]

Next, DEM is expected to be positively related to SESRVOTES. Kimenyi and Tollison (1995) provide evidence suggesting that more complex legislation and larger spending packages are both positively related to longer sessions. Democrat legislators generally prefer larger spending packages, and, therefore, will be willing to invest in the necessary time to provide these fiscal benefits to their constituents. Similarly, GGDP is the relative size of the public budget and captures the "complexity" of legislation produced, as in Kimenyi and Tollison (1995).[3] It (GGDP) is therefore expected to be positively related to SESRVOTES. Lastly, given that a possible tendency exists for the length of proceedings to vary across periods of a Presidential term, PREZ is included, and it is equal to one for Presidential election years (and zero otherwise). It is noted that the model presented above in equation (4.1) is quite parsimonious. This is important because decomposition of the means differences (i.e., the difference in the length of Senate sessions before and after C-SPAN2) requires interacting the C-SPAN dummy with all other regressors in the model. This procedure uses valuable degrees of freedom in our small sample. It is also necessary, however, that the model be correctly specified to perform such decomposition tests (Jackson and Lindley, 1989). These ideas are detailed further below.

Again, data for the regressions are annual and cover the extended period 1972-2001 (n=30). Given that C-SPAN2 began covering Senate sessions in 1986, a comparable number of observations are represented before and after C-SPAN2. Means and standard deviations for the variable series are reported in Table 4.1. Although many scientific time series are stationary, quite

### Table 4.1 Summary Statistics

| Variable | Mean | Standard Deviation |
|----------|------|--------------------|
| SESRVOTES | 0.388 | 0.081 |

### Table 4.1 Summary Statistics (Continued)

| Variable | Mean | Standard Deviation |
|----------|------|--------------------|
| CSPAN | 0.533 | 0.507 |
| DEM | 0.527 | 0.061 |
| PREZ | 0.267 | 0.450 |
| GGDP | 21.067 | 1.550 |

often time series data are trending (Kennedy, 1998: 264; Nelson and Plosser, 1982; Enders, 1995). Our concern here is with using a time variant endogenous variable with time *in*variant regressors (see Trevino, Daniels, Arbelaez and Upadhyaya, 2002). Therefore, several diagnostic techniques were used to check for stationarity (or trends) in the dependent variable, SESRVOTES. A correlogram, or graphical plot of the autocorrelation coefficients for SESRVOTES suggests that this variable series is stationary (Kennedy, 1998; Box and Jenkins, 1970). In addition, we conducted various unit root tests to check for stationarity. These include the Augmented Dickey-Fuller test (ADF) and the Phillips-Perron (PP) test. Test statistics for these are reported in Table 4.2. The ADF test (Dickey and Fuller, 1979) is the most commonly

### Table 4.2 Unit Root Tests on SESRVOTES [*]

| | Augmented Dickey-Fuller Test | Phillips-Perron Test |
|----------|------------------------------|----------------------|
| SESRVOTES | -3.45* | -3.40* |

[*]    * indicates the 0.10 level of significance for the test statistic, or better.

used test in the literature (see Mixon, Sawyer and Upadhyaya, 2002; Elder and Kennedy, 2001), and the ADF test result—using critical values in MacKinnon (1990)—presented in Table 4.2 fails to reject the null hypothesis of "stationarity." The PP test (Phillips, 1987; Phillips and Perron, 1988) uses non-parametric correction to deal with any correlation in the error terms. It also fails to reject the null hypothesis of "stationarity" of the SESRVOTES series. These results indicate that using SESRVOTES in its level form is not problematic.

Results from two Ordinary Least Squares (OLS) estimations of equation (4.1) are presented in Table 4.3. In both models, the coefficient for C-SPAN is positive (0.088) and significant at the

Table 4.3 OLS and Autoregressive Error Regression Results dependent variable: SESRVOTES [*]

|  | OLS Models | | AE Models | |
|---|---|---|---|---|
|  | *(1)* | *(2)* | *(3)* | *(4)* |
| constant | 0.478* | 0.478* | 0.489* | 0.492* |
|  | (2.57) | (2.62) | (2.22) | (2.28) |
| CSPAN | 0.088* | 0.088* | 0.083* | 0.084* |
|  | (3.89) | (3.97) | (2.99) | (3.08) |
| DEM | -0.473* | -0.474* | -0.433 | -0.438 |
|  | (-2.52) | (-2.58) | (-1.91) | (-1.98) |
| PREZ | -0.004 |  | -0.007 |  |
|  | (-0.15) |  | (-0.34) |  |
| GGDP | 0.005 | 0.005 | 0.004 | 0.004 |
|  | (0.77) | (0.78) | (0.48) | (0.48) |
| F-statistic | 7.95* | 11.00* |  |  |
| R-square | 0.56 | 0.56 | 0.43 | 0.43 |
| RESET F-statistic | 2.675 | 2.682 |  |  |
| Durbin-Watson *d* | 1.527 | 1.537 | 1.799 | 1.822 |
| LM F-test | 0.173 | 0.214 |  |  |

[*] Notes: The numbers in parentheses above are *t*-statistics. * indicates the 0.05 level (or better) of significance.

0.05 level or better. These results suggest that annual U.S. Senate sessions are about 63 minutes longer per recorded vote in the C-SPAN2 era (i.e., 1986 and beyond).[4] This result is consistent with the idea that Senate incumbents are able to use various parliamentary procedures (e.g., filibustering) to create and extend debates in order to take advantage of the presence of television cameras. Such exposure would be expensive for challengers to replicate (Mixon, 2002; Mixon, 2001). Given a recent reporting that the administrative cost of session time in a Congressional chamber is $7,000 per hour (Bill Press, CNN's *Cross-fire*, 1999), the C-SPAN parameter (0.088) suggests that the presence of C-SPAN2 has increased administrative costs in the Senate by $7,392 per recorded vote (based on a 12 hour day). With the 1997-1998 recorded vote total of 612, it is estimated that C-SPAN2 increased administrative costs in the U.S. Senate during the 105th Congress by $4.53 million. This estimate is quite comparable to the average from 1972-1996 reported in Mixon et al. (2001) of $3.33 million (1998 dollars). It is also comparable to their own estimate for the increase in administrative costs in the Senate due to C-SPAN2 for the 104th Congress (1995-1996). That figure is about $3.05 million.

Returning to Table 4.3, in both OLS models, DEM is negative and significant. The parameter estimate suggests that an increase in DEM of one percentage point reduces the amount of U.S. Senate session time spent per recorded vote by about 3 minutes. The sign of this parameter is contrary to the expectation discussed above, although a similar result using different data and estimation techniques was found by Mixon et al. (2001). Lastly, neither GGDP nor PREZ is significant at usual levels in the OLS versions.

Many linear regression models are mis-specified; that is, they suffer biases due to irrelevant variables, omitted variables, errors in measurement and other problems. Ramsey's RESET (Ramsey, 1969) is a general test for all types of specification error, such as those listed above. In versions (1) and (2) of Table 4.3, a RESET fails to reject the null hypothesis of "no specification error." Additionally, given the macro-political economy model tested here, a check for heteroscedastic residuals was performed. Given that OLS assumes constant error variance, heteroscedasticity would lead to inefficient OLS estimates. We performed a test for heteroscedastic residuals in Breusch and Pagan (1979) and Engle (1982). This is a Lagrange multiplier test, and it is reported for versions (1) and (2) of Table 4.3 as the LM F-test. In both cases, our computed test statistic fails to reject the null hypothesis of "homoscedastic errors."

Despite the fact that the Durbin-Watson *d* statistics reported in Table 4.3 fail to reject the null hypothesis of "no autocorrelation," and the fact that SESRVOTES appears to be stationary (see discussion above), we re-ran the OLS models using an Autoregressive Error Model (AE) for comparison. These results are presented as versions (3) and (4) in Table 4.3. The parameter estimates in these two versions are very close to their OLS counterparts. The CSPAN parameter is 0.083 and 0.084 in the two versions; this compares well with the two estimates of 0.088 in versions (1) and (2) of the table. DEM retains a negative sign, though it is marginally *in*significant in the two AE models. The other variables—PREZ and GGDP—retain the same signs and approximately the same significance levels as they do in the OLS versions.

## 4.3 Additional Statistical Exploration

As pointed out above, decomposing the means for the pre- and post-C-SPAN2 eras employs interaction terms, and thus consumes valuable degrees of freedom given our relatively small sample size. As the RESET F-statistic suggests, version (2) of Table 4.3 provides an unbiased and parsimonious regression equation for use in a statistical decomposition exercise (Jackson and Lindley, 1989). Interaction effects are used to more fully understand C-SPAN2's role in increasing the length of Senate proceedings (per recorded vote). An approach that employs interactions, as described by Jackson and Lindley (1989), is one that partitions the group means difference (i.e., the *total effect*) into components that measure the *structural effect* and the *residual effect*.[5] Beyond these, the subcomponents of the residual effect—the *constant effect* and the *coefficient effect*—are measured to provide a more accurate picture of C-SPAN2's importance.

The mean for SESRVOTES in the C-SPAN2 era (i.e., 1986-2001) is 0.4365, while its mean during the pre-C-SPAN2 era (i.e., 1972-1985) is 0.3319. The total effect is the difference in the these two means, or 0.1046. Given the results in Table 4.3 regarding the CSPAN parameter, U.S. Senate proceedings are significantly longer in the C-SPAN2 era; that is, the total effect is significantly different from zero (at the 0.05 level; see Table 4.3). The structural effect indicates how the length of Senate proceedings would differ across the two eras under similar circumstances.[6] To calculate the structural effect, we obtained parameter estimates for the version (2) of Table 4.3 regression using only the post-C-SPAN2 era data (i.e., 1986-2001). This, of course, necessitates omitting CSPAN on the right hand side of the equation. Once this equation is estimated, mean values for DEM and GGDP from the pre-C-SPAN2 era only (i.e., 1972-1985) are plugged into the expression, and a predicted value for SESRVOTES is obtained. In this case that value is 0.4420, suggesting that the average value for SESR-VOTES during the 1972-1985 period would have been 0.4420 had C-SPAN2 cameras (or legislative television) been present during that period. The structural effect is the actual average for the C-SPAN2 period (0.4365) minus the prediction for the 1972-1985 period in the presence of television (0.4420). Here, the structural effect is -0.0055, comprising -5% (approximately) of the total effect. Any difference across the two regimes under similar technological circumstances (i.e., legislative television in both regimes) is due to explanatory factors out-side of the scope of our investigation. However, the remaining sub-component of the total effect—the *residual effect*—is equal to the prediction of 0.4420 used above to calculate the structural effect minus the mean value of SESRVOTES during the *pre*-television era (0.3319). This calculation suggests that the mean for SESRVOTES during the 1972-1985 period would have been 0.4420 in the presence of C-SPAN cameras, but instead the actual mean was 0.3319 (in the absence of television). The difference, 0.1101, represents the residual effect and it constitutes 105% of the total effect. The positive residual effect indicates that C-SPAN2 has had a positive influence on U.S. Senate session time (per recorded vote). This effect (0.1101) is significant at the 0.01 level based on an F-statistic of 8.527 (3, 25 degrees of freedom).

Because the residual effect alone can be an ambiguous measure in determining C-SPAN2's role in increasing Senate session time, its sub-components are estimated (Jackson and Lindley, 1989). The first of these is the *constant effect*, which measures the *direct* impact C-SPAN2 has on official Senate time per recorded vote. The constant effect is the estimated coefficient for CSPAN in version (2) of Table 4.3, with the addition of interaction terms (CSPAN•DEM and CSPAN•GGDP). The constant effect is interpreted as the effect C-SPAN2 has on the intercept term of the U.S. Senate session length function, and a significant finding *unambiguously* indicates that C-SPAN2 plays an important role in shaping session length (Jackson and Lindley, 1989). The constant effect has an unexpected sign in this case (-0.345), although it is not significant at acceptable levels (based on a *t*-statistic of -0.80). Lastly, the coefficient effect measures the *indirect* impact C-SPAN2 has on Senate session time. This indirect effect occurs through C-SPAN2's interaction with the other regressors in the model (i.e., DEM and GGDP). The coefficient effect is interpreted as the effect C-SPAN2 has on the slope of the U.S. Senate session length function, however a significant finding leaves room for ambiguity still (Jackson and Lindley, 1989). The coefficient effect is equal to the residual effect minus the constant effect. Here it is 0.4551, and it is significant at about the 0.08 level based on an F-statistic of 3.258 (2, 25 degrees of freedom). All of our decomposition estimates are presented below in Table 4.4.

**Table 4.4 Decomposition Measures for C-SPAN2's Impact on U.S. Senate Session Length** [*]

| Total Effect | Structural Effect | Residual Effect | Constant Effect | Coefficient Effect |
|---|---|---|---|---|
| 0.1046** | -0.0055 | 0.1101*** | -0.3450 | 0.4551* |
| (2.62) | | [8.527] | (-0.80) | [3.258] |

[*]  Notes: [1] The numbers in parentheses above are *t*-statistics; those in brackets are F-statistics. [2] The *t*-statistic given for the Total Effect is taken from the CSPAN parameter estimate in version (2) of Table 4.3; the other *t*-statistic and F-statistics are computed as in Jackson and Lindley (1989). No statistical testing was performed for the estimate of the Structural Effect. [3] ***(**)[*] denotes the 0.01(0.05)[0.10] level of significance.

How are our findings regarding the constant and coefficient effects to be interpreted? As Jackson and Lindley (1989: 522) point out in their review of discrimination studies in the labor economics literature,

> "Regardless of the magnitude of the point estimate of the residual difference, a significant appropriately signed constant effect...indicates discrimination. Ambiguity occurs when the constant effect is not significant and the coefficient effect is appropriately signed and significant. When this occurs, the statistical significance of discrimination hinges crucially on the strength of the theoretical basis underlying the model."

Our interpretation of the results is, of course, that the positively signed and significant *residual* and *coefficient effects* are indicative of the notion that C-SPAN2 has played a key role in increasing U.S. Senate session time (per recorded vote). That incumbent Senators can use the cameras as low-cost advertising (that would be expensive for challengers to replicate) is an idea that fits nicely into the vote- and utility-maximizing models of legislator behavior in public choice theory. Our tests, therefore, provide more definitive statistical evidence regarding the positive impact legislative television has on legislative session lengths.

## 4.4 Concluding Comments

Although voters can, perhaps, make more informed decisions in the presence of legislative television, this chapter points out that there are some ancillary consequences which come from recent trends to televise the political process. Given the institutional rules in the U.S. Senate, the presence of cameras on the legislative floor allows for political grandstanding and posturing that might not take place otherwise. As such, the cameras contribute to longer proceedings—an estimated 63 minutes more per recorded vote—in the U.S. Senate, as incumbents use that chamber's parliamentary procedures as low-cost advertising. The administrative cost to taxpayers of this added time is not trivial, amounting to perhaps as much as $3 million per Congress. Given the impact of technology on the conduct of legislatures, and the resulting cost to taxpayers based on this conduct, perhaps policy makers and academics should (re-)consider the proposed constitutional reforms to deal with the impact of developments in telecommunications on government that are detailed in Crain and Goff (1988).

## Notes to Chapter 4

1. The "productivity" index approach is both less problematic and intuitively more interesting than using annual proceedings length (in days) alone as the dependent variable.

2. Mixon, Gibson and Upadhyaya (2003) detail anecdotally and statistically how the presence of C-SPAN2 cameras impacts the use, by vote-maximizing incumbent Senators, of various parliamentary procedures in the Senate (e.g., filibustering) as low-cost forms of advertising. Mixon et al. (2001) make use of empirical studies on the effectiveness of political advertising and other forms of campaigning. These include Banaian and Luksetich (1991), Bender (1988), Lott (1991), Erikson and Palfrey (1993), Mueller and Stratmann (1994), and Nagler and Leighley (1992). Mixon et al. (2001) also employ studies indicating

factors leading to the significant advantage incumbents have in the electoral process. Prominent among these is the seminal study by Mayhew (1974). Our thesis (in this chapter) also emanates from these earlier studies.

3. Larger government often follows from a legislative session involving an extensive logrolling process that results in complex spending packages, such as *Omnibus Appropriations* bills.

4. This prediction is based on a 12-hour day, given that the dependent variable is measured as days per recorded vote in the Senate.

5. This partitioning or decomposition technique has proved helpful in labor market studies that examine racial or gender discrimination on wages using race or gender dummy variables. See Jackson and Lindley (1989) for a survey of this literature.

6. See Jackson and Lindley (1989) for a concise description of the decomposition technique and all of the relevant formulae and statistical tests.

# Chapter 4 References

Banaian, K. and W.A. Luksetich (1991) "Campaign spending in congressional elections," *Economic Inquiry* 29: 92-100.

Bender, B. (1988) "An analysis of congressional voting on legislation limiting congressional campaign expenditures," *Journal of Political Economy* 96: 1,005-1,021.

Box, G.E.P. and G.M. Jenkins (1970) *Time series analysis: Forecasting and control*, San Francisco, CA: Holden Day.

Breusch, T.S. and A.R. Pagan (1979) "A simple test for heteroscedasticity and random coefficient variation," *Econometrica* 47: 1,287-1,294.

*Congressional Quarterly Almanac* (1972-2001), Washington, D.C.: CQ, Inc.

Crain, W.M. and B.L. Goff (1988) *Televised legislatures: Political information technology and public choice*, Boston, MA: Kluwer Academic Publishers.

Dickey, D.A. and W.A. Fuller (1979) "Distribution of the estimators for autoregressive time series with a unit root," *Journal of the American Statistical Association* 74: 427-431.

Elder, J. and P.E. Kennedy (2001) "Testing for unit roots: What should students be taught?" *Journal of Economic Education* 32: 137-146.

Enders, W. (1995) *Applied econometric time series*, New York, NY: John Wiley & Sons, Inc.

Erikson, R.S. and T.R. Palfrey (1993) "The spending game: Money, votes and incumbency in congressional elections," Cal Tech Social Science Working Paper 851.

Engle, R.F. (1982) "Autoregressive conditional heteroscedasticity with estimates of the variance of United Kingdom inflation," *Econometrica* 50: 987-1,007.

Jackson, J.D. and J.T. Lindley (1989) "Measuring the extent of wage discrimination: A statistical test and a caveat," *Applied Economics* 21: 515-540.

Kennedy, P. (1998) *A guide to econometrics*, Cambridge, MA: The MIT Press.

Kimenyi, M.S. and R.D. Tollison (1995) "The length of legislative sessions and the growth of government," *Rationality and Society* 7: 151-155.

Krehbiel, K. (1998) *Pivotal politics: A theory of U.S. lawmaking*, Chicago, IL: University of Chicago Press.

Lott, J.R., Jr. (1991) "Does additional campaign spending really hurt incumbents? The theoretical importance of past investments in political brand name," *Public Choice* 72: 87-92.

MacKinnon, J. (1990) "Critical values for cointegration tests," Working Paper, University of California at San Diego.

Mayhew, D. (1974) "Congressional elections: The case of vanishing marginals," *Polity* 6: 295-317.

Mixon, F.G., Jr. (2002) "Does legislative television alter the relationship between voters and politicians?" *Rationality and Society* 14: 109-128.

Mixon F.G., Jr., M.T. Gibson and K.P. Upadhyaya (2003) "Has legislative television changed legislator behavior? C-SPAN2 and the frequency of Senate filibustering," *Public Choice*, forthcoming.

Mixon, F.G., Jr., D.L. Hobson, and K.P. Upadhyaya (2001) "Gavel-to-gavel congressional television coverage as political advertising: The impact of C-SPAN on legislative sessions," *Economic Inquiry* 39: 351-364.

Mixon, F.G., Jr., W.C. Sawyer and K.P. Upadhyaya (2002) "Unit root test popularity among economists: Sampling the literature," *Economia Internazionale* 55: 37-46.

Mueller, D.C. and T. Stratmann (1994) "Informative and persuasive campaigning," *Public Choice* 81: 55-77.

Nagler, J. and Leighley (1992) "Presidential campaign expenditures: Evidence on allocations and effects," *Public Choice* 73: 319-333.

Nelson, C.R. and C.I. Plosser (1982) "Trends and random walks in macroeconomic time series," *Journal of Monetary Economics* 10: 139-162.

Phillips, P.C.B. (1987) "Time series regression with unit roots," *Econometrica* 55: 277-301.

Phillips, P.C.B. and P. Perron (1988) "Testing for a unit root in time series regression," *Biometrica* 75: 335-346.

Ramsey, J.B. (1969) "Tests for specification errors in classical linear least-squares regression analysis," *Journal of the Royal Statistical Society* 31: 350-371.

*Statistical Abstract of the United States* (various issues), U.S. Bureau of the Census, Washington, D.C.

Trevino, L.J., J.D. Daniels, H. Arbelaez and K.P. Upadhyaya (2002) "Market reform and foreign direct investment in Latin America: Evidence from an error correction model," *International Trade Journal* 16: 367-392.

# 5

## *"Mr. Speaker, I Ask Unanimous Consent to Address...":* *C-SPAN and the Value of One Minute Speeches*

*"Fame-seeking, celebrity, and fandom are deeply rooted psychological phenomena, existing in most societies, but they are amplified and facilitated by commercial market economies and modern technologies...Today, television, the compact disk, and the Internet give fans further assistance in finding, following, and enjoying their stars from a distance...Ours is an economy of fame. Our culture is about the commodification of the individual and the individual image." (Cowen, 2000: 8)*

### 5.1 Introduction

The previous chapter provided statistical evidence suggesting that the presence of C-SPAN2 cameras has significantly increased annual session time per recorded vote in the U.S. Senate. In doing so, it lends credence to earlier work (Mixon, Hobson, and Upadhyaya, 2001) indicating that C-SPAN(2) cameras have increased two-year U.S. House *and* U.S. Senate proceedings time per bill. The findings also directly addresses the Crain-Goff (1988) question: *has legislative television mattered?*

In Chapter 4, we presented a review of prior work along with new estimates (see Chapter 4) as support for a theoretical model positing that C-SPAN(2) cameras serve incumbent federal legislators as a medium for low-cost advertising. Such exposure, as we previously explain, would cost substantial sums of money for challengers to replicate, giving incumbent legislators a significant electoral advantage. This chapter addresses one source of advertising exposure available to U.S. Representatives—one minute speeches. In fact, we posit here that the presence of legislative television at the federal level has increased the value of this parliamentary procedure by impacting the ability of representatives to reach wide audiences through grandstanding and posturing on salient political issues. In this chapter, we present new evidence that is consistent with this hypothesis.

## 5.2 Television and One Minute Speeches in the U.S. House

Although we are not concerned primarily with the broader cultural implications of live television in the legislative arena, our supposition that legislative television matters to politicians and constituents fits neatly into the broader discussion of fame and fame-seeking in Cowen (2000). According to Cowen (2000: 51):

> "Successful politicians must use television and compete with popular culture for audience attention. Leaders therefore court voters by entertaining them and making them feel good. This strategy may increase popularity and win votes…"[1]

The one minute speeches period in the U.S. House provides one avenue for the type of competitive exposure Cowen refers to above. One minute speeches are short speeches (no more than 300 words) that may be made by Representatives before or after legislative business each day. Any member may seek recognition to make a speech on a subject of his or her choice, though not exceeding one minute in duration. One minute speeches are often coordinated through the leadership's *Theme Team* (in each Party) to focus on particular topics, but the speeches often are not limited to such topics. Participants in the *Theme Team* effort usually receive priority seating and recognition.[2]

The one minute speeches period is granted at the discretion of the Speaker of the U.S. House, as are the number of such speeches. Some days one minute speeches may be limited to 15 for each side, while on other days they are unlimited (The Congressional Institute, 2002; U.S. House Committee on Rules Majority Office, 2002). To give a one minute speech, Representatives go to the front row of seats on their Party's side and sit down. The Speaker will recognize Members in turn, beginning with the majority Party. Any Representative wishing to deliver a one minute speech stands to seek recognition, and addresses the Chair by saying: "Mr. Speaker, I ask unanimous consent to address the House for one minute and to revise and extend my remarks."

Members are strongly recommended to recognize *House Rule XVII* ("Of Decorum and Debate"). This rule prohibits members from referring directly to the television audience, from using offensive language in speaking about the President, and from characterizing any Senate action/inaction or making reference to any individual member of the Senate. Within these limitations, some Representatives have become more recognized (and popular) through skillful use of this procedure. Some have even gained recognition by skirting these limitations. Mixon, Hobson and Upadhyaya (2001: 352-353) describe such a story relating to Special Order speeches.

> "On 19 May 1999, Representative David McIntosh (R-IN) led a colloquy on the House floor with several other Republican Representatives in early prime time during the Special Order session of House business. They were describing in coversational tone what they viewed as the radical environmental views of then-Vice President Al Gore. Passages from Gore's book on global warming were

read aloud [mockingly] before the C-SPAN cameras. CNN's *Cross-fire* repeatedly broke away [from its live coverage] to cover the colloquy, and liberal cohost Bill Press complained about such a use of taxpayer money on the House floor."

Surely Representative McIntosh and the others stood to gain politically by C-SPAN's presence.

Perhaps the most recognized one minute speech artisan has been former Representative James Traficant (D-OH). A sample of five one minute speeches given by Traficant highlight his use of sarcasm, humor, and irony. These are:

### The Economy [June 10, 1997]

"Mr. Speaker, if this economy is so great, why are American workers losing their jobs? If this economy is so great, why are American workers going bankrupt in record numbers? If that is not enough to massage your Dow Jones, check this out: If this economy is so great, why do many families need three jobs just to pay their bills? Let us tell it like it is: When you hold this economy up to your nosey, this economy does not smell so rosy…I yield back all the propaganda on this great economy."

### Social Security [September, 30, 1999]

"Mr. Speaker, Social Security is in trouble…Congress has tried GrammRudman, budget caps, lockboxes, and now some in Congress even want to create a zodiac ploy of a 13th month. Beam me up, Mr. Speaker. Let us be honest. As long as Social Security money is there, available to be spent, it will be spent, by both Parties…"

### Regulations Cost Taxpayers [October 12, 1999]

"Mr. Speaker, *The Gettysburg Address* is 286 words. *The Declaration of Independence* is 1,322 words. Government regulations on the sale of cabbage is 27,000 words. Mr. Speaker, now if that's not enough to stuff your cabbage roll, regulations cost taxpayers $400 billion in a year, $4,000 per every family each and every year…Beam me up, Mr. Speaker. I yield back 2,800,000 words in our tax code."

### Chinese Relations [November 11, 1999]

"Mr. Speaker, reports say the White House will support China over Taiwan, communism over democracy. Unbelievable. The report says the White House will put tough conditions on it. Like what, Mr. Speaker? A waiting period on Chinese missile launches? A promise that China will not sell any of their stolen technology at missile shows? How about trigger locks on all those Chinese missiles? Beam me up, Mr. Speaker. These cerebral constipators have already given away the farm."

### Accidental Hospital Deaths [July 26, 2000]

"Mr. Speaker, accidental deaths caused by doctors and hospitals in America [have] reached 120,000 per year. Meanwhile, gun deaths have dropped 35 percent. In fact, accidental gun deaths dropped to 1,500 last year. Think about it. We have hospitals slicing and dicing American people like Freddie Kruger, and Congress is passing more gun laws. Beam me up. There is something wrong in America when one is 80 times more likely to be killed by a doctor than [by a] Smith & Wesson…Maybe we need a gun in surgery. I yield back the fact that the Second Amendment was not written just to cover duck hunters."

These speeches cover everything from domestic regulation to foreign relations. Dates on the three speeches provided from 1999 indicate just how active Representative Traficant was with regard to one minute speeches. Again, this is only a small sampling of his effort in this particular area. Traficant used the one-minute speech masterfully in portraying himself as a maverick in Congress, expressing his views with hallmark phrases and intonations. The well-known *Star Trek* phrase—"Beam me up…"—became an identifying mark of a Traficant one-minute speech. Many one minute speeches end before sixty seconds, and the speakers "yield back the balance" of the minute (to the Chair). Traficant's one minute speeches often ended on a facetious note, such as when he "yield[ed] back" 2.8 million words in the U.S. tax code.

The examples above also highlight another idea presented in this book, namely that some parliamentary procedures are useful (at times) to legislators by giving them a venue for grandstanding or posturing on popular issues. Traficant's citation of decaying employment statistics and his warning of problems with the Social Security system would be certain to resonate with union workers and retirees in his Ohio district. Implicitly taking a position against the anti-gun lobby, as in the final speech above, would appeal to the many moderate Democrats and conservatives residing in his district. Lastly, warnings of Chinese missile proliferation is a perennially salient issue to a national constituency.

That Traficant became a political icon in America is evidenced by the many Internet sites devoted to recording/displaying the text of his (many) one minute speeches.[3] He is one of many Representatives that used one minute speeches or Special Order speeches to gain the name recognition that is so important to incumbents (Mayhew, 1974; Lott, 1991; Mueller and Stratmann, 1994), as in the epigraph to Chapter 3 in this book. The following equation offers a test of the hypothesis that legislative television has enhanced the value, and hence the use, of parliamentary procedures such as the one minute speech in the U.S. House:

(5.1) $ONEMIN = \alpha + \beta ELECT + \delta PREZ + \gamma DEMC + \varepsilon$.

ONEMIN is equal to the number of one minute speeches made by all U.S. Representatives during various two-month periods (data on the total number of one minute speeches come from the Congressional Research Service). Optimally, data both before 1982 and after 1982 would be used to estimate the impact of C-SPAN on the use of one minute speeches in the House. The CRS, however, maintains a data series that begins in 1985. We collected data on the number of one minute speeches given by all U.S. Representatives during the September-October period in the even-numbered years, as well as those made in the February-March period of the odd-numbered years. We also chose to concentrate on the 10-year period following the introduction of full-time C-SPAN coverage of House proceedings (i.e., 1983-1992). The first two years (1983 and 1984), however, fall out of our sample given the data limitation mentioned above. Therefore, ONEMIN is equal to the total number of one minute speeches given in September-October of the even years (i.e., 1986, 1988, 1990, and 1992), and the total number of one minute speeches given in February-March during the odd years (i.e., 1985, 1987, 1989, and 1991).[4] This construction of ONEMIN provides one minute speeches information for two-month periods before and after each general election of U.S. Representatives in the time frame studied.[5]

ELECT is a dummy variable equal to one for the even years—the U.S. House election years—and zero otherwise. At least one prominent factor points to a negative expectation for this variable. Although Congress is usually in session for approximately the same amount of time during each of these two-month periods, prior research has shown that Congress is more active legislatively in the first year of a Congress, or the odd year of a Congress (see Havrilesky, 1995; Mixon and Upadhyaya, 2002).[6] One would, therefore, predict more one minute speeches and other forms of political participation during the February-March periods of the odd years, as new and old members of Congress develop a fresh legislative agenda.

Mixon, Gibson and Upadhyaya (2003) provide a competing hypothesis for ONEMIN. They point out that the C-SPAN cameras enhance the value (to incumbents) of various parliamentary procedures in the re-election process, such as one minute speeches, given that they can be used to broadcast a Representative's views on a myriad of issues to thousands of potential voters. If this hypothesis is true, even-numbered years could exhibit larger values for ONEMIN than odd-numbered years, given the proximity of September-October to the general election (i.e., the first Tuesday in November). We expect the coefficient for $\beta$ to be positive, thus supporting the hypothesis that the low-cost advertising medium made possible by C-SPAN cameras has increased the value and use of parliamentary procedures in the U.S. House, especially preceding a general election.

PREZ and DEMC are control variables. PREZ is equal to one for presidential election years, and zero otherwise. DEMC is a dummy variable equal to one for years wherein the Democrats controlled both houses of Congress, and zero otherwise. It is possible that Representatives spend more time in their districts campaigning during the Presidential election season. This could be due to in-district visitations by the incumbent President (i.e., the coat-tail effect) or Presidential challenger. In this case, $\delta$ will retain a negaive sign. Unified government, as in the case where DEMC equals one, could embolden the opposition Party, thus leading to more one minute speeches in a particular year. In many cases, one minute speeches and other parliamentary procedures are the most effective and efficient way for the minority Party to have its message heard by voters and its ideologies revealed to political action committees (see Dempster and Westley, 2000). In this case, $\gamma$ will be positive. Finally, $\alpha$ is the intercept of equation (5.2), and $\varepsilon$ is a random error term.

Summary statistics (means and standard deviations) for the four variables listed in equation (5.1) are presented in Table 5.1. Table 5.1 also includes OLS regression estimates of equation

### Table 5.1 Summary of OLS Results
### dependent variable: ONEMIN [509.00, 217.24] *

|  | Version (1) | | Version (2) | |
|---|---|---|---|---|
|  | *coefficient* | *t-value* | *coefficient* | *t-value* |
| constant | 298.30** | 2.24 | 446.5*** | 5.15 |
| ELECT [0.50, 0.53] | 367.4** | 2.58 | 318.0** | 2.12 |
| PREZ [0.25, 0.46] | -484.8** | -2.78 | -386.0** | -2.23 |

### Table 5.1 Summary of OLS Results
### dependent variable: ONEMIN [509.00, 217.24] (Continued)[*]

|  | Version (1) | | Version (2) | |
|---|---|---|---|---|
|  | coefficient | t-value | coefficient | t-value |
| DEMC [0.75, 0.46] | 197.6 | 1.39 | | |
| R-square | 0.6934 | | 0.5456 | |
| adj. R-square | 0.4634 | | 0.3639 | |

[*]   Notes: The numbers in brackets above are means and standard deviations for the respective variable. For the regression coefficients, ***(**) denotes the 0.01(0.05) level of significance for a one-tailed test (Leamer, 1978; Kennedy, 1998). RESET F-statistics (Ramsey, 1969) for the regressions above could not be obtained due to a linear combination constraint.

(5.1). Of the three regressors, ELECT and PREZ are significant at the 0.05 level. The variable of interest, ELECT, has the expected sign and is significantly related to ONEMIN. Its coefficient suggests that, *ceteris paribus*, one minute speeches activity is greater just prior to the election (i.e., in September-October) than just after a new Congress convenes (i.e., February-March), despite research indicating that the first year of a Congress exhibits significantly more legislative activity than the second year (i.e., the election year). The size of the coefficient—or 367.4—is quite large. This value is about 72.2 percent of the mean value for ONEMIN and suggests that there are 367 additional one-minute speeches made during the typical (two-month) election season relative to the beginning of each new Congress, *ceteris paribus*. This effectively increases U.S. House session time by 367 minutes over this two-month period. Using the $7,000 per hour cost estimate provided by Bill Press of CNN's *Crossfire* mentioned in the previous chapter, this translates into an added expense to taxpayers of $42,817 (in 1998/99 dollars) for this two-month period alone.

The version (2) result is also supportive of version (1), with ELECT retaining a positive (318.0) and significant parameter estimate. Again, the coefficient for ELECT is large, representing about 62.5 percent of the mean for ONEMIN. The cost estimate for this *ceteris paribus* increase in House session time of 318 minutes for September/October is $37,100 (in 1998/99 dollars). Each of the OLS regression equations produces a high degree of explanatory power, with R-square values ranging from 0.5456 to 0.6934. As with the previous chapter on the length of Senate sessions, we explore decomposition measures of the one-minute speeches average in our sample.

The average number of one minute speeches for September-October in the election years is 571.5, compared to just 446.4 for February/March in the off (odd) years. The difference—125—represents the *total effect* (see previous chapter). Using data from election years only and a specification of equation (5.1) including only DEMC and PREZ, we predicted the number of one minute speeches for the February-March observations under the assumption that a Congressional election immediately followed this two-month period; this considers the September-October and February-March periods under similar circumstances. To do this, we substituted the mean values for DEMC and PREZ from the odd years into a regression equation using these two variables and the election (even) year data only. Our prediction is 888.25, suggesting that the average for ONEMIN for February-March would have been 888.25 had this time period preceeded a general election, as does September-October. The difference between the election year average of 571.5 and this prediction of 888.25 is -316.75, and constitutes the *structural effect*. As in the previous chapter, any observed difference here in election year and odd-year one minute speeches totals (for the two-month periods observed) is due to factors not included in, nor relevant to, this study.

The structural effect is useful, however, for estimating the *residual effect*, which might offer some evidence that C-SPAN's presence has enhanced the value of one minute speeches as low-cost advertising. As such, a greater incidence of one minute speeches activity would be expected in the even-year periods, despite the fact that congressional activity is generally greater in the odd years (Havrilesky, 1995). The residual effect is the prediction of 888.25 used to obtain the structural effect minus the average of ONEMIN for the odd-year months (February-March). Here, that value is 446.5. This difference—the residual effect—is 441.75. A cost estimate for the added one minute speeches produced during the election season (i.e., September-October of even years), using the residual effect, is $51,538 (1998/99 dollars).

The two subcomponents of the residual effect—the *constant effect* and *coefficient effect*—are also estimated and tested against the null hypothesis that each is equal to zero (Jackson and Lindley, 1989). The constant effect is the estimated dummy for ELECT from a re-estimation of version (1) estimation in Table 5.1 *plus* the two interaction terms (i.e., ELECT•PREZ and ELECT•DEMC). The constant effect here is 70.50, however it is not significant at usual levels. The coefficient effect is equal to the residual effect minus the constant effect. Here it is 371.25. These decomposition measures are all presented in Table 5.2.

**Table 5.2 Decomposition Measures for ELECT's Impact on One-Minute Speeches Frequency** [*]

| Total Effect | Structural Effect | Residual Effect | Constant Effect | Coefficient Effect |
|---|---|---|---|---|
| 125.00*** | -316.75 | 441.75** | 70.50 | 371.25* |
| (2.58) |  | [8.787] | (0.76) | [4.007] |

[*]   Notes: [1] The numbers in parentheses above are *t*-statistics; those in brackets are F-statistics. [2] The *t*-statistic given for the total effect is taken from the ELECT parameter estimate in version (2) of Table 5.1; the other *t*-statistic and F-statistics are computed as in Jackson and Lindley (1989). In this case, however, F-statistics for our decomposition measures are not *exact*, given linear combination problems with one of the interaction terms in the estimation procedure. The procedure we used to calculate the two F-statistics produced upward biased estimates. [3] No statistical testing was performed for the estimate of the structural effect. [4] ***(**)[*] denotes the 0.05(0.075)[0.15] level of significance (Ramanathan, 1998).

Once again we are left with a correctly signed and significant residual effect (see note [2] to Table 5.2). This finding is, however, an ambiguous indicator of C-SPAN's importance (Jackson and Lindley, 1989). As in the previous chapter, we also find a positive but insignificant constant effect, coupled with a positive and (marginally) significant coefficient effect (see note [2] to Table 5.2).[7] We are again left with the difficult task of interpreting our decomposition tests, given that "…[a]mbiguity occurs when the constant effect is not significant and the coefficient effect is appropriately signed and significant. When this occurs, the statistical significance of discrimination hinges crucially on the strength of the theoretical basis underlying the model (Jackson and Lindley, 1989: 522)." As in the previous chapter, our interpretation of the results is that the positively signed and significant *residual* and *coefficient effects* are consistent with the notion that C-SPAN has played a key role in increasing the value of parliamentary procedures such as one-minute speeches in the U.S. House. Prior to the advent of legislative television, one minute speeches represented a part of the Congressional record available to constituents at high cost, such as by searching the Internet or by visiting a local research/government depository library and perusing the printed records. In the absence of television, one minute speeches would represent a high-cost form of information for voters, and Representatives would likely seek other avenues for garnering votes during election cycles. In a pre-television era, there would *likely* have been greater use of one-minute speeches during the more legislatively active first year (odd year) of each Congress (see Havrilesky, 1995; Mixon and Upadhyaya, 2002). With television, one minute speeches have become an avenue for incumbents to reach distant constituents at low cost—an effort that would be expensive for challengers to replicate.

Of course, these results are taken from statistical testing using very few observations, and thus limited degrees of freedom, among other problems noted above. Additionally, the lack of data both before and after the advent of legislative television requires that we interpret the sign/significance of the election-year dummy variable as indicative of the value of C-SPAN coverage. The suggestion that C-SPAN cameras enhance the value of one minute speeches in the House, and thus legislators' use of this parliamentary tool for re-election purposes, is palatable to public choice theory. However, our ability to statistically determine the "C-SPAN portion" of the increased use of one minute speeches in election years (or even years) is, at best, difficult. Therefore, to provide more definitive evidence of the impact of legislative television on the value, and thus use, of parliamentary procedures, the next chapter turns once again to the U.S. Senate to review recent research of incumbents' use of the filibuster procedure.

## Notes to Chapter 5

1. Cowen (2000), the author of the epigraph to this chapter, goes on to point out that fame-seeking by politicians diminishes the stock of moral authority that a leader can wield. The increasing weight of short-run political opinion makes politicians, especially the President, a moral follower rather than a moral leader. "The media…promote political images that will attract viewers, rather than images that support the dignity of the office. (Cowen, 2000: 51)." It would be interesting to examine, more comprehensively than is done in Cowen (2000) or other works, the political ethos in America since the adoption of C-SPAN(2) coverage near the end of the 20th century (see also Cowen, 2002). This could be done, perhaps, by extending the work of Ehrenhalt (1991), Sutter (1998), and Clark and Lee (2001).

2. Information on one minute speeches is available at the Congressional Institute and the U.S. House of Representatives Committee on Rules (Majority Office). These sources are used extensively in this chapter.

3. Representative Traficant was expelled from the U.S. House in 2002 by a two-thirds majority vote. The political decision was made in light of bribery, racketeering, and tax evision convictions of Traficant. As such, he is only the second person expelled since the Civil War (cnn.com). His example provides support for Cowen's (2000) point that the media-intense strategies pursued by government officials in the era of (entertainment) television dimishes respect for public office and

the stock of moral authority a leader can wield. As Cowen (2000: 54) puts it, "…politics increasingly attracts the career politician. Politics will be full of the dishonest, although the high degree of scrutiny will check their ability to act dishonestly…a society with commercialized fame, and thus intense media scrutiny, does not generate great leaders…it [instead] produces and attracts individuals who are adept at currying public favor and avoiding public blame."

4. We thank Jay Morris of the U.S. House Clerk's office and Jennifer Manning of the Congressional Research Service for providing us with one-minute speeches data.

5. ONEMIN contains only discrete, integer values (i.e., count data). However, as Table 5.1 points out, the mean for ONEMIN is 509, and it ranges from 322 to 1,012 for the two-month periods (i.e., February/March and September/October) for our time frame (1985-1992). Given such large values, discreteness is not a practical issue here, and it is not modeled as in Cameron and Trivedi (1998), Zelterman (1999), and Winkelmann (2000).

6. October and March are months with approximately the same number of calendar and legislative days. Although September is a longer month than February, the Labor Day break taken by Congress leads to about as many legislative days in September as February.

7. We use the term "marginal" here given that the coefficient is found to be significant at only the 0.14 level (approximately). However, both Leamer (1978) and Kennedy (1998) suggest relaxing the usual requirements in statistical testing in the presence of such small samples.

# Chapter 5 References

Cameron, A.C. and P.K. Trivedi (1998) *Regression analysis of count data*, Cambridge, U.K.: Cambridge University Press.

Clark, J.R. and D.R. Lee (2001) "Optimal trust in government," *Eastern Economic Journal* 27: 19-34.

*Congressional Quarterly Almanac* (1985-2001), Washington, D.C.: CQ, Inc.

Cowen, T. (2000) *What price fame?* Cambridge, MA: Harvard University Press.

Cowen, T. (2002) *Creative destruction: How globalization is changing the world's cultures*, Princeton, NJ: Princeton University Press.

Crain, W.M. and B.L. Goff (1988) *Televised legislatures: Political information technology and public choice*, Boston, MA: Kluwer Academic Publishers.

Dempster, G.M. and C. Westley (2000) "Who gets the goods? Moderate voting records, diminishing returns, and PAC contributions," *Economics and Politics* 12: 321-333.

Ehrenhalt, A. (1991) *The United States of Ambition: Politicians, power and the pursuit of office*, New York, NY: Times Books.

Havrilesky, T. (1995) *The pressures on American monetary policy*, Boston, MA: Kluwer Academic Publishers.

Jackson, J.D. and J.T. Lindley (1989) "Measuring the extent of wage discrimination: A statistical test and a caveat," *Applied Economics* 21: 515-540.

Kennedy, P. (1998) *A guide to econometrics*, Cambridge, MA: The MIT Press.

Leamer, E.E. (1978) *Specification searches: Ad hoc inference with nonexperimental data*, New York, NY: John Wiley.

Lott, J.R., Jr. (1991) "Does additional campaign spending really hurt incumbents? The theoretical importance of past investments in political brand name," *Public Choice* 72: 87-92.

Mayhew, D. (1974) "Congressional elections: The case of vanishing marginals," *Polity* 6: 295-317.

Mixon, F.G., Jr., M.T. Gibson and K.P. Upadhyaya (2003) "Has legislative television changed legislator behavior? C-SPAN2 and the frequency of Senate filibustering," *Public Choice*, forthcoming.

Mixon, F.G., Jr., D.L. Hobson and K.P. Upadhyaya (2001) "Gavel-to-gavel congressional television coverage as political advertising: The impact of C-SPAN on legislative sessions," *Economic Inquiry* 39: 351-364.

Mixon, F.G., Jr. and K.P. Upadhyaya (2002) "Examining legislative challenges to central bank autonomy: Macroeconomic and agency cost models," Unpublished Manuscript, The University of Southern Mississippi.

Mueller, D.C. and T. Stratmann (1994) "Informative and persuasive campaigning," *Public Choice* 81: 55-77.

Ramanathan, R. (1998) *Introductory econometrics with applications*, New York, NY: The Dryden Press.

Ramsey, J.B. (1969) "Tests for specification errors in classical linear least-squares regression analysis," *Journal of the Royal Statistical Society* 31: 350-371.

Sutter, D. (1998) "Media scrutiny and the quality of politicians," Unpublished Manuscript, University of Oklahoma.

Winkelmann, R. (2000) *Econometric analysis of count data*, Berlin: Springer-Verlag.

Zelterman, D. (1999) *Models for discrete data*, Oxford, U.K.: Clarendon Press.

# 6

# Legislative Television and Extended Debates in the U.S. Senate: A Survey of Prior Research

*"Live legislative television has introduced an innovative way for voters to make up their minds about electing legislators…The conduct of legislative sessions…ha[s also] adjusted to the new voter-legislator relationship that has been created by legislative television." (Crain and Goff, 1988: 65)*

## 6.1 Introduction

In Chapter 4 we provided new empirical estimates consistent with a theoretical model positing that C-SPAN(2) cameras serve incumbent federal legislators as a medium for low-cost advertising. Such exposure, as we previously indicated, would require (perhaps) large sums of money for political challengers to combat, giving incumbent legislators an important electoral advantage. The previous chapter addresses one source of advertising exposure available to U.S. Representatives—one minute speeches. There we present empirical evidence consistent with the idea that the presence of legislative television at the federal level has increased the value (usefulness) of this particular parliamentary procedure in the U.S. House. This chapter reviews previous published work on a similarly valuable tool in the U.S. Senate, namely the filibuster procedure (see Mixon, Gibson and Upadhyaya, 2003; Mixon, 2002). We pay particularly close attention to some of the statistical evidence presented in this prior research on filibustering. Much of this evidence supports our primary hypothesis.

## 6.2 Television and Filibustering in the U.S. Senate

As we stated in the previous chapter, although we are not concerned primarily with the broader cultural implications of live television in the legislative arena, our supposition that legislative television matters to politicians and their constituents fits neatly into the discussion of fame and fame-seeking in Cowen (2000). As Cowen (2000: 51) explains, successful politicians use television to compete for audience attention. The filibuster procedure in the U.S. Senate may provide an additional avenue for the type of competitive exposure referred to by Cowen (2000). Filibustering, however, is not as intuitively straightforward as the one minute speeches procedure given that it usually involves opposition to specific bills and resolutions that come before the Senate. That means that filibustering is often more organized and structured along party lines (Mixon, Gibson and Upadhyaya, 2003).

As Mixon et al. (2003) point out, since the adoption of its *Rule 22* in 1917, the U.S. Senate has had a clearly stipulated parliamentary procedure for terminating *extended debate* (such as a filibuster) and bringing to a vote the motion at hand. This procedure is called *cloture*.[1] Consistent with our thesis and that in Mixon et al. (2003), Binder and Smith (1997) point out that Senators' true views on filibustering are predominantly "political," not "principled." As such, it can be stated that legislators care less about procedures than about the procedures' bearing on policy outcomes (Krehbiel, 1998; Mixon et al., 2003).[2] Binder and Smith (1997) also fail to find evidence that the filibuster is a "moderaring" institution, nor that most filibusters (historically) arose from Southern opposition to civil rights legislation. As Mixon et al.

(2003) explain, these ideas are all consistent with the notion that Senators would be expected to employ the filibuster procedure with greater frequency in the presence of televised legislative (U.S. Senate) sessions. To this supposition, Mixon et al.'s only addition is the idea that, out of many issues, legislators care about procedures' impact on expected utility (i.e., vote production), and that the presence of television in the U.S. Senate changes the value of the filibuster procedure to Senate incumbents seeking re-election.[3]

Many of the ideas above are supported by an anecdotal construct in Mixon et al. (2003). There, the story of HR2646—a bill proposing to expand the benefits of educational savings accounts (established in 1997)—is summarized. The House bill was shepherded into the U.S. Senate in 1998. As Mixon et al. (2003) point out, the bill was opposed by then President Bill Clinton, and fellow Democrat Senator Carol Moseley-Braun (D-IL). Several features of the story are relevant here. First, 1998 was an election year, and Carol Moseley-Braun was thought to be the most vulnerable Democrat incumbent seeking re-election. Second, education was thought to be the most salient issue to American voters in 1998, and Moseley-Braun's alternative plan to spend $22 billion in federal money on local school construction was thought to be quite popular. Therefore, television coverage by C-SPAN2 and other media of Moseley-Braun's speeches/debates on this issue/plan were expected to increase her popularity and, thus, her re-election prospects (see Mixon et al., 2003). Lastly, that the Democrats decided to implement their filibuster plan against a significant likelihood that the alternative Republican plan would eventually pass in the Senate suggests that C-SPAN2 coverage is often thought of as a low-cost outlet for persuasive campaigning on salient issues. Moseley Braun's actions between the Fall of 1997 and June of 1998—against the likelihood of Senate passage of the Republican plan—are consistent with this view (see Mixon et al., 2003). The Mixon et al. anecdote serves, therefore, as a useful example of legislative television's power to enhance the information-providing capacity of (i.e., the advertising value of) various parliamentary procedures in the federal legislature.

## 6.3 Filibustering in the Early Stages of C-SPAN2

Two recent studies have analyzed the impact of legislative television on filibustering in the U.S. Senate. Both of these have equated cloture motions with filibustering, as explained above. In one of these, Mixon (2002) identifies six key bills that were filibustered during the 99th Congress (1985-1986). These are included below in Table 6.1. In all, non-leadership Senators

### Table 6.1 Bills "Filibustered" During the 99th Congress [*]

| |
|---|
| Line-Item Veto |
| Debt Limit/Balanced Budget |
| Washington Airports Transfer |
| Hobbs Act Amendment |
| Military Aid to the Contras |
| Omnibus Drug Bill |

[*]    Source: Mixon (2002).

from 10 different states, representing a mix of both political parties, played important roles in structuring/organizing these 6 filibusters. Using these filibuster attempts, Mixon (2002: 110) "concentrates on whether voters respond to the increased exposure of politicians [through filibustering] by 'tuning in' [to C-SPAN2 coverage, and]...whether the actions of legislators themselves are directly tied to voter viewership." To do so, Mixon (2002) empirically links the simultaneous relationship between per-capita C-SPAN2 subscribership (potential viewership) and the probability that Senators employ one of the showcasing or persuasive grandstanding parliamentary procedures available in the U.S. Senate, namely the filibuster. Use of the 1985-1986 data also reveals insights into how voters and Senators viewed the presence of legislative television (C-SPAN2) in its early stages. As Mixon (2002: 118) suggests:

"As a testable hypothesis, one would expect that…[C-SPAN2] viewership varies directly with the degree of legislative 'activity' exhibited by…Senators if voters view legislative television as an innovative information-gathering device. Also, one would expect that the probability of the incidence of legislative 'activity' (e.g., filibuster[ing]) would be greatest in those areas (states) where the return to filibustering as a form of *persuasive* advertising are potentially the greatest (i.e., where viewership is the greatest)."

Mixon (2002), therefore, uses a two-equation system to test these hypotheses. This system is:

(6.1) VIEW = $f$(RINC, METRO, PVOTE, DIVIDE, FILIB)

and,

(6.2) FILIB = $f$(REPS, DEMS, VIEW).

VIEW denotes C-SPAN2 subscribership per voting age population (for 1986) in each of the 50 states, while FILIB is a dummy variable for the 10 states represented by filibustering Senators regarding the six filibusters listed in Table 6.1. As Mixon (2002) points out, both dependent variables are also represented on the right hand side of the opposite equation; that is, they are both regressors in the other statistical expression. This feature suggests that the equations (models) are to be estimated simultaneously. Next, the presence of FILIB, a binary variable, on the left hand side of (6.2) indicates the need for probit estimation, while the continuous measure of VIEW on the left hand side of (6.1) suggests the use of OLS.[4]

We concentrate here on the two variables of interest—FILIB on the right hand side of (6.1), and VIEW on the right hand side of (6.2). Results concerning these two variables are summarized in Table 6.2, along with other regression statistics. As the contents of Table 6.2

**Table 6.2 Parameter Estimates from Mixon's (2002) Simultaneous Probit Model** [*]

|  | Equation (6.1) OLS | Equation (6.2) Probit |
|---|---|---|
| FILIB | 0.013 | |
| VIEW | | 41.96* |
| R-square | 0.21 | 0.11 |
| $\sigma_{12}$ | 0.003* | |

[*]     Note: The cells above contain parameter estimates, where * denotes statistical significance.
Source: Mixon (2002).

indicate, a greater propensity of a U.S. Senator to "filibuster" leads to increased viewership of Senate proceedings by that Senator's constituents, though not significantly so. However, a (potentially) larger viewing audience among a Senator's constituency is positively and significantly related to the propensity of that state's Senators to effect a filibuster. Although the first finding fails to statistically support the notion that legislative activity works to shape political viewership in a way hypothesized, the second finding is consistent with the notion that "*persuasive* filibustering (or 'grandstanding') provides senators with a low-cost form of campaign advertising (Mixon, 2002: 123-125)." In fact, a marginal increase in C-SPAN2 viewership in a state (VIEW) increases the probability of observing a filibustering Senator in that state (FILIB) by about 14 percentage points. Both equations produce reasonably large R-square statistics for cross-sectional data, and the estimated covariance between the residuals in (6.1) and (6.2), noted as $\sigma_{12}$, supports the notion that the probability of legislative filibustering activity is positively related to the (potential) size of the viewing audience. This evidence—that filibuster activity is positively related to the number of potential viewers of C-SPAN2, and thus positively related to the potential electoral rewards from political grandstanding (i.e., votes)—lends credence to the work presented in the previous chapter on one minute speeches in the U.S. House of Representatives. Given the unusually small data sample employed in Chapter 5, supporting evidence from Mixon (2002) is important in providing further empirical evidence of our hypothesis that legislative television enhances the persuasive advertising value of certain parliamentary procedures in the U.S. Congress. Next we turn to additional evidence on filibustering activity from Mixon et al. (2003).

## 6.4 Filibustering in the U.S. Senate: Time Series Evidence

Mixon et al. (2003) expand the work of Mixon, Hobson and Upadhyaya (2001), Crain and Goff (1986 and 1988), and the results presented in this book by examining the frequency of Senate filibusters over a 40 year time horizon (1959-1998), which includes a period of C-SPAN2 coverage (1986-1998). As Mixon et al. (2003) point out, if the parliamentarian need for cloture can be used as low-cost advertising by incumbent politicians who are maximizing expected utility (i.e., vote production), a greater incidence of filibusters (or filibuster threats) would be expected in the legislative television era of the U.S. Senate. On the other hand, if the *real* cost of filibusters (e.g., lost work time on other legislation, lost time on the hustings, etc.) is too often prohibitive, or if with increased media exposure (C-SPAN2) a smaller amount of filibustering would accomplish more regarding vote production (i.e., an output effect), the filibuster frequency in the Senate is not likely to be altered, or may even fall, in the presence of television cameras in the Senate chamber (Mixon et al., 2003).

As a test of the hypothesis above, Mixon et al. (2003) collect data on the number of cloture votes occurring annually in the U.S. Senate from 1959-1998.[5] This count becomes the dependent variable (CVOTES) in their regression model. Among other regressors measuring the number of bills and resolutions presented in the U.S. Senate each year, the presence (absence) of a Democrat Party majority in the Senate (each year), the presence of a filibuster-proof majority (of either Party) in the Senate (each year), the presence of unified government (i.e., political party of the President and Senate majority are the same), total federal government spending as a percent of GDP (each year), and a variable denoting the number of votes required to invoke cloture in the U.S. Senate (each year), Mixon et al. (2003) make use of a dummy variable equal to one for the the presence of C-SPAN2 cameras, and zero otherwise. This variable (CSPAN) takes the value of zero from 1959 to 1985, and it is equal to one from 1986 to 1998. As they state, if C-SPAN2 enhances the value of filibustering as low-cost advertising (for incumbents only), it is expected that the number of filibusters would be positively related to the presence of television coverage. In this case, one would expect CSPAN to be positively related to CVOTES in their model.

Table 6.3 presents the actual filibuster count for the ten years preceeding C-SPAN2 coverage and for the 10 years following C-SPAN2 coverage. The data in Table 6.3 represent a subset of

**Table 6.3 Pre- and Post-C-SPAN2 Filibuster Count in the U.S. Senate [*]**

| Pre-C-SPAN2 Era (Year): | Filibuster Count: |
|---|---|
| 1976 | 4 |
| 1977 | 5 |
| 1978 | 8 |
| 1979 | 4 |
| 1980 | 17 |
| 1981 | 7 |
| 1982 | 19 |
| 1983 | 7 |
| 1984 | 12 |
| 1985 | 9 |

### Table 6.3 Pre- and Post-C-SPAN2 Filibuster Count in the U.S. Senate (Continued)[*]

| Post-C-SPAN2 Era (Year): | Filibuster Count: |
|---|---|
| 1986 | 14 |
| 1987 | 23 |
| 1988 | 20 |
| 1989 | 9 |
| 1990 | 15 |
| 1991 | 20 |
| 1992 | 28 |
| 1993 | 20 |
| 1994 | 22 |
| 1995 | 21 |

[*]    Source: Data taken from Mixon et al. (2003) study, though not originally presented in that study.

the data used by Mixon et al. (2003). A cursory look at these data clearly reveals that filibustering was more common in the first 10 years after C-SPAN2 than in the 10 years immediately preceeding the network's coverage of the U.S. Senate. The first 10 years produce an average of 9.2 filibusters per year, with a standard deviation of 5.25. The latter 10 years produce a much larger average—19.2 filibusters per year—and a standard deviation of 5.31, which is quite similar to that from the 1976-1985 period. Filibuster count statistics from 1996, 1997 and 1998—the last three years of the Mixon et al. (2003) data set are even more remarkable. They are, respectively, 29, 24 and 29, and produce an annual average of 27.33 (with a standard deviation of 2.89). The filibuster count during the Kennedy-Johnson Administrations (1961-1968) produces an average of 2.5 filibusters per year, with a standard deviation of 1.69. This finding is consistent with the suggestion in Binder and Smith (1997), that most filibusters (historically) did not arise from Southern opposition to civil rights legislation.

A cursory look at filibuster frequencies at various times in history does not constitute a statistical test. To explore C-SPAN2's impact on filibustering, Mixon et al. (2003) estimate a regression equation utilizing CVOTES (the annual filibuster count in the Senate from 1959-1998) as the dependent variable, and CSPAN—the C-SPAN2 dummy variable described above—along with the other measures detailed above as regressors.[6] In four separate Poisson specifications, each passing a Regression Specification Error Test (see Ramsey and Gilbert, 1972), Mixon et al. (2003) report a positive and significant parameter for the C-SPAN2 dummy variable. This result indicates that, *ceteris paribus*, the annual filibuster count in the post-C-SPAN2 era (after 1985) is significantly larger than that before 1986, supporting the view that legislative television serves incumbent legislators as an avenue for low-cost advertising in their quest for re-election.

Mixon et al. (2003) also suggest, as we have in the previous chapters, that the simple dummy variable approach is limited in its ability to predict that C-SPAN2 has played a direct role in increasing the filibuster count over time in the U.S. Senate. What is needed is an unrestricted regression approach wherein the C-SPAN2 dummy variable is interacted with other variables in the model. As we explain above, this approach allows for the partitioning of the group means difference (i.e., the total effect) into subcomponents. The primary subcomponent of the total effect—the residual effect—and its two subcomponents, the constant and coefficient effects, are all explained in great detail in the preceding chapters. Therefore, we will not reiterate those explanations here. We do point out, however, that Mixon et al.'s (2003) estimate for each of these measures is both positive and statistically significant. As they point out, although a positively signed/significant residual effect can be an ambiguous indicator of C-SPAN2's importance in increasing the use of the filibuster procedure, the positive/significant constant effect unambiguously indicates that C-SPAN2 has played a direct role in increasing the use of filibustering by U.S. Senators. Additionally, the positive/significant coefficient effect suggests that the presence of legislative television has also had a positive effect on filibustering through its interaction with the other regressors in the model.

Some of the *predicted* filibuster count data are presented in Table 6.4, following the pre-

**Table 6.4 Pre- and Post-C-SPAN2 *Predicted* Filibuster Count in the U.S. Senate** [*]

| Pre-C-SPAN2 Era (Year): | *Predicted* Filibuster Count: |
|:---:|:---:|
| 1976 | 12.1796 |
| 1977 | 5.2747 |
| 1978 | 7.5138 |
| 1979 | 8.2895 |
| 1980 | 12.1823 |
| 1981 | 10.9197 |
| 1982 | 13.0763 |
| 1983 | 10.8675 |
| 1984 | 10.2464 |
| 1985 | 11.2120 |
| Post-C-SPAN2 Era (Year): | *Predicted* Filibuster Count: |
| 1986 | 16.8963 |
| 1987 | 18.7000 |
| 1988 | 22.5247 |
| 1989 | 20.8793 |
| 1990 | 25.0757 |
| 1991 | 22.1579 |

**Table 6.4 Pre- and Post-C-SPAN2 *Predicted* Filibuster Count in the U.S. Senate (Continued)[*]**

| 1992 | 23.4214 |
|------|---------|
| 1993 | 12.4160 |
| 1994 | 14.1469 |
| 1995 | 24.3302 |

[*] Source: Predicted values taken from Mixon et al. (2003) Poisson model (version 1), though not originally presented in that study.

and post-C-SPAN2 era format of Table 6.3. These data can be compared with the actual filibuster count data presented in Table 6.3. The mean value for the *predicted* filibuster count for the 10 years preceeding C-SPAN2 is 10.1762 (with a standard deviation of 2.4320). This is much lower than the mean value for the *predicted* filibuster count for the 10 years immediately following the implementation of C-SPAN2 (see data in Table 6.4). In the latter period, the mean is 20.0548 (with a standard deviation of 4.3601). The *predicted* filibuster count statistics for 1996, 1997 and 1998—the last three years of the Mixon et al. (2003) data set—are larger. They are, respectively, 26.1967, 21.3617 and 25.8933, and produce an annual average of 24.4839 (with a standard deviation of 2.7082). Lastly, the *predicted* filibuster count during the Kennedy-Johnson Administrations (1961-1968) produces an average of 3.8698 filibusters per year, with a standard deviation of 1.2068. As with our cursory look at the actual data above, this finding is consistent with the suggestion in Binder and Smith (1997), that most filibusters (historically) did not arise from Southern opposition to civil rights legislation. Even though Mixon et al. (2003) aim to examine the economic determinants of filibustering from 1959-1998, their model does reasonably well in *predicting* the actual filibuster count during that period (as the data comparisons above and in the tables suggest). These overall results, taken from a relatively large annual time series, provide further support for the inferences drawn from the one minute speeches regression results detailed in the previous chapter.

# 6.5 Concluding Comments

The decomposition tests results from Mixon et al. (2003) suggest that the use of the Senate's *Rule 22*—which allows for filibustering—has increased significantly in the presence of C-SPAN2 (legislative) television cameras. Such a use of procedures by incumbent legislators—an important element in the effort to achieve re-election—has at least two results. First, Senate sessions are likely to become longer and costlier for taxpayers to fund. This has been shown by Mixon, Hobson and Upadhyaya (2001), and our own empirical work presented in Chapter 4. Second, given that such posturing and positioning on the issues through the filibuster procedure by incumbent Senators is costly for challengers to replicate, the likelihood of incumbents' electoral success is increased, *ceteris paribus*. This conclusion is empirically tested, and verified, in the next chapter of this book. Both of these results support the public choice model of the political process.

# Notes to Chapter 6

1. Stages of the legislative process subject to filibustering include the motion to proceed to consideration of a bill, consideration of amendments to a bill or of a bill itself, motions to go to conference, and the passage of the conference report. See Krehbiel (1998) for more on the mechanics of filibustering.

2. See Krehbiel (1998) and Beth (1995) for more on cloture motions and the filibuster procedure. Mixon et al. (2003: fn 7) also explain that there is no entry in government documents or Congressional records recorded as "filibusters" or "filibustering." This makes documenting the frequency of this activity somewhat problematic. Mixon et al. (2003: fn 7) argue that use of cloture motions, which are recorded, serves as a viable proxy. They argue that "if the 'demand' for extended debate is increased due to the presence of C-SPAN2, then the 'demand' for cloture [votes] is also increased."

3. Mixon et al. (2003) also point out that any political information provided by legislators through the use of filibusters (on C-SPAN2) is generally positive for the inbumbent filibustering Senator. They also recognize that there are necessary conditions for a filibuster to occur. First, given the importance of party unity, the value of a filibuster to a political party (or a group at large) must be positive. With small majorities, the marginal benefit/cost of a one-member change in the legislative body can be significant. Second, with a filibustering party, the existence of individuals who would benefit is necessary for a filibuster to occur. On any given bill, these individuals will likely represent a small group of Senators. See Mixon et al. (2003) for additional discussion of the likely impact of C-SPAN2 on the *number* of Senators who might benefit from any individual filibuster, and the nominal and real costs of filibustering. Lastly, our insertion above of the parenthetical phrase "a group at large" allows for the possibility that filibustering might benefit legislative groups other than those comprised of members of a political party. These include membership organizations such as the Congressional Black Caucus (Mixon and Ressler, 2001; Mixon and Chittom, 2003; Chittom and Mixon, 2003) and the U.S. Senate Centrist Coalition (Mixon, Ressler and Gibson, 2003).

4. See Maddala (1983) and Mixon (2002) for a more complete description of the simultaneous probit model.

5. As stated previously, the existence of a filibuster is a matter of interpretation. Mixon et al. (2003) use cloture votes as a proxy.

6. The presence of a discrete count dependent variable and time series data requires careful specification choices. After checking for equidispersion of the dependent variable, stationarity for all variables employed, and the absence of serial correlation, Mixon et al. (2003) choose a Poisson specification. For additional references on this model, see Greene (1997), Kennedy (1998), Cameron and Trivedi (1998), Zelterman (1999), and Winkelmann (2000). For additional references

on stationarity/serial correlation issues, see Dickey and Fuller (1979), Nelson and Plosser (1982), Phillips (1987), Phillips and Perron (1988), Enders (1995), Kennedy (1998), Mixon, Sawyer and Upadhyaya (2002), Breusch (1978), Godfrey (1978), Davutyan (1989), and Baltagi (1999).

## Chapter 6 References

Baltagi, B.H. (1999) *Econometrics*, Berlin: Springer-Verlag.

Beth, R.S. (1995) "What we don't know about filibusters," Congressional Research Service, Typescript.

Binder, S.A. and S.S. Smith (1997) *Politics or principle? Filibustering in the United States*, Washington, D.C.: Brookings Institute Press.

Breusch, T.S. (1978) "Testing for autocorrelation in dynamic linear models," *Australian Economic Papers* 17: 334-355.

Cameron, A.C. and P.K. Trivedi (1998) *Regression analysis of count data*, Cambridge, UK: Cambridge University Press.

Chittom, A.B. and F.G. Mixon, Jr. (2003) "Do congressional leaders detect and deter cartel cheating? Evidence from committee assignments," *Economics of Governance*, forthcoming.

Cowen, T. (2000) *What price fame?* Cambridge, MA: Harvard University Press.

Crain, W.M. and B.L. Goff (1986) "Televising legislatures: An economic analysis," *Journal of Law and Economics* 29: 405-421.

Crain, W.M. and B.L. Goff (1988) *Televised legislatures: Political information technology and public choice*, Boston, MA: Kluwer Academic Publishers.

Davutyan, N. (1989) "Bank failures as Poisson variates," *Economics Letters* 29: 333-338.

Dickey, D.A. and W.A. Fuller (1979) "Distribution of the estimators for autoregressive time series with a unit root," *Journal of the American Statistical Association* 74: 427-431.

Enders, W. (1995) *Applied econometric time series*, New York, NY: John Wiley & Sons, Inc.

Godfrey, L.G. (1978) "Testing against general autoregressive and moving average error models when regressors include lagged dependent variables," *Econometrica* 46: 1,293-1,302.

Greene, W.H. (1997) *Econometric analysis*, Upper Saddle River, NJ: Prentice-Hall.

Kennedy, P. (1998) *A guide to econometrics*, Cambridge, MA: The MIT Press.

Krehbiel, K. (1998) *Pivotal politics: A theory of U.S. lawmaking*, Chicago, IL: University of Chicago Press.

Maddala, G.S. (1983) *Limited dependent and qualitative variables in econometrics*, New York, NY: Cambridge University Press.

Mixon, F.G., Jr. (2002) "Does legislative television alter the relationship between voters and politicians?" *Rationality and Society* 14: 109-128.

Mixon, F.G., Jr. and A.B. Chittom (2003) "Are Congressional Black Caucus members more reliable? Loyalty screening and committee assignments of newly elected legislators," *The American Journal of Economics & Sociology*, forthcoming.

Mixon, F.G., Jr., M.T. Gibson and K.P. Upadhyaya (2003) "Has legislative television changed legislator behavior? C-SPAN2 and the frequency of Senate filibustering," *Public Choice*, forthcoming.

Mixon, F.G., Jr., D.L. Hobson and K.P. Upadhyaya (2001) "Gavel-to-gavel congressional television coverage as political advertising: The impact of C-SPAN on legislative sessions," *Economic Inquiry* 39: 351-364.

Mixon, F.G., Jr. and R.W. Ressler (2001) "Loyal political cartels and committee assignments in Congress: Evidence from the Congressional Black Caucus," *Public Choice* 108: 313-330.

Mixon, F.G., Jr., R.W. Ressler and M.T. Gibson (2003) "Congressional Memberships as Political Advertising: Evidence from the U.S. Senate," *Southern Economic Journal*, forthcoming.

Mixon, F.G., Jr., W.C. Sawyer and K.P. Upadhyaya (2002) "Unit root test popularity among economists: Sampling the literature," *Economia Internazionale* 55: 37-46.

Nelson, C.R. and C.I. Plosser (1982) "Trends and random walks in macroeconomic time series," *Journal of Monetary Economics* 10: 139-162.

Phillips, P.C.B. (1987) "Time series regression with unit roots," *Econometrica* 55: 277-301.

Phillips, P.C.B. and P. Perron (1988) "Testing for a unit root in time series regression," *Biometrica* 75: 335-346.

Ramsey, J.B. and R. Gilbert (1972) "A Monte Carlo study of some small sample properties of tests for specification error," *Journal of the American Statistical Association* 67: 180-186.

Winkelmann, R. (2000) *Econometric analysis of count data*, Berlin: Springer-Verlag.

Zelterman, D. (1999) *Models for discrete data*, Oxford, UK: Clarendon Press.

# 7

## *The Advertising Effect of Television Coverage on Legislative Turnover: Evidence from the U.S. House of Representatives*

*"When we last wrote about Marge Roukema, the New Jersey Republican was running for her life against a...primary opponent. The latest news is that she's called in the big-money calvary to prevent the...unthinkable precendent that a Congressional incumbent might actually lose...The dirty little secret of the 2000 fight for House Control is that only 30 seats out of 435 are even competitive..." (The Editor, The Wall Street Journal, June 1, 2000: A22)*

## 7.1 Introduction

This chapter partially fills the void in the economics literature concerning the impact of television on the democratic process by concentrating on the effect of television on legislative turnover at the federal level in the United States. This chapter employs data from the U.S. House of Representatives during the period 1946-1994, part of which the U.S. House received significant television coverage by the C-SPAN cable network. As with Crain and Goff (1988) and the empirical work presented thus far in this book, we use the voter-shopping construct, which views political services as search/experience goods. This dichotomy, as explained in Chapter 2, emerges from a series of works by Nelson (1970 and 1974), and is based largely on the economics of information described in a seminal paper by Stigler (1961).

In this chapter we also include a description of some of the previous work on the incumbency advantage in politics. Much of this work details the prequisites received by incumbent legislators. These advantages are linked to the low turnover rates exhibited historically in American federal legislative politics (some of this work is mentioned briefly in the notes to Chapter 4 of this book). We follow this discussion with the presentation of a public choice model of legislative turnover.

## 7.2 Previous Literature on Advertising and Incumbency Advantage

A series of studies on incumbency advantage has appeared in the public choice literature over the past three decades. Mayhew (1974) points out that incumbents in the U.S. House are made safer from defeat by the increased name recognition that is the result of franked mailings to district residents. In fact, the mail-flow curve closely tracks the incumbency advantage curve drawn from existing data before 1974 (Mayhew, 1974). Second, as it has become easier to reshape congressional lines, it follows that federal politicians would attempt to redraw lines in a way that ensures incumbent success (Mayhew, 1974). In other passages of the same editorial containing the epigraph to this chapter, the editor of *The Wall Street Journal* attributes incumbent security in the U.S. House to gerrymandering (reshaping Congressional district borders). Although Mayhew attaches less importance to this aspect, a recent study by Mixon and Upadhyaya (1997) suggests that the 1982 amendments to the *Voting Rights Act of 1965* gained support precisely because of the external incumbency effects accruing to non-black

Democrats and Republicans who benefitted from the redistricting that resulted in a larger number of black-majority districts. In fact, they report that turnover in those states that redesigned districts based on racial composition were about 10.3 percentage points lower in 1988 than for those that did not re-shape Congressional lines, *ceteris paribus*.

Third, Mayhew (1974) points out that incumbent legislators often take advantage of more scientific polling data and techniques available to them. This allows incumbents to achieve a proper alignment of political views with constituents in their own districts. Finally, increasing within-district government spending represents a perennial advantage to incumbents (Mayhew, 1974). This last point is supported by the empirical work of Fiorina (1977), who goes further by pointing out that veteran incumbent representatives have the added advantage of being able to expedite the bureaucratic process in Washington for their constituents. Although the Mayhew study is not without its critics (see Erikson, 1971; Ferejohn, 1977), all of the aspects listed above are unique to incumbents, and, to a large extent, are determined within the federal legislative process. The Mayhew-Fiorina "behavioral explanation" is also supported in work by Krehbiel and Wright (1983).

In addition to recent research that supports a statistical relationship between political advertising and electoral success (Banaian and Luksetich, 1991; Nagler and Leighley, 1992), Mueller and Stratmann (1994) use a Downsian spatial model to analyze the types of political advertising that occur in election settings (see Downs, 1957). According to these authors, *informative* advertising by a candidate provides information about his or her own positions, or those of his or her opponent. As such, informative advertising expenditures by Candidate A substitute, at least partially, for the same type of expenditures of Candidate B.[1] These authors also suggest that with regard to *persuasive* advertising—which is an attempt to convince voters to provide support regardless of platforms or positions—that because both candidates are trying to convince voters that they are honest and will bring programs to the district, it is the candidate who is *perceived* to be more honest and able to provide more for the district who stands to win. This candidate is likely to be the one who has spent the most money convincing voters that he or she has these attributes (Mueller and Stratmann, 1994: 65). The Mueller-Stratmann study has implications concerning the types of media outlets and media time that incumbents have access to (such as C-SPAN) for engaging in political advertising. The institutional arrangements of the U.S. House of Representatives—one minute speeches and Special Order speeches—are tailored to impacting voter beliefs in this type of persuasive manner. Previous chapters in this book have shown a greater propensity among legislators to (1) use one minute speeches during election seasons, and (2) consume large of amounts of legislative session time per recorded vote. Support for the advertising-votes relationship is important to the hypothesis that, with the advent of television coverage, federal representatives will use the low-cost C-SPAN medium in a way that provides advantages over potential challengers. In the next section, we present our statistical model of legislative turnover and the empirical results.

## 7.3 Statistical Model and Results

Based on the literature described above, the following equation is proposed as a test of our theory:

(7.1) $\text{TURN} = \alpha + B_1\text{QUIT} + B_2\text{INFL} + B_3\text{RGNP} + B_4\text{CSPAN} + \varepsilon.$

The definitions of all variables included in equation (7.1) are provided in Table 7.1. The dependent variable in equation (7.1) is the turnover rate (% form) in the U.S. House of

### Table 7.1 Variables, Definitions, Means and Standard Deviations *

| Variable | Definition | Mean | Std. Deviation |
|---|---|---|---|
| TURN | Turnover rate (% form) in the U.S. House of Representatives from 1946-1994. The percent of the House represented by newly elected Representatives. | 16.17 | 5.12 |
| QUIT | Percentage of incumbents in the House that choose *not* to seek re-election in a given two-year election cycle preceding each TURN. | 8.65 | 2.42 |
| INFL | The sum of inflation rates over each two-year election cylce (% form) preceding each TURN. | 8.68 | 6.17 |
| RGNP | The *real* GNP growth rate in the U.S over over each two-year election cycle (% form) preceding each TURN. | 4.72 | 5.50 |
| CSPAN | dummy variable equal to one for each two-year election cycle offering House television coverage by C-SPAN (1982 and thereafter), and zero otherwise | 0.28 | 0.46 |

\* Sources: [1] *Economic Report of the President* (various issues), [2] *Historical Statistics of the United States* (1970), [3] Ornstein, Mann and Malbin (1992), [4] Pearce (1991), [5] *Statistical Abstract of the United States* (various issues), [6] Will (1992), and [7] C-SPAN website (www.cspan.org).

Representatives for the period 1946-1994. It represents the percentage of the U.S. House comprised of newly elected Representatives in each election cycle. QUIT is the percentage of incumbents in the U.S. House choosing *not* to seek re-election during any given election cycle (i.e., they retire, they seek other office, etc.). As such, "quits" directly lead to newly-elected Representatives. Therefore, QUIT is expected to be positively related to TURN.

INFL and RGNP are statistical measures of the macroeconomy that might impact incumbents' re-election prospects. INFL is the sum of inflation rates (P*) over each two-year election cycle. Because this variable is particularly egregious from the point of view of citizen-voters, as it increases one would expect that legislative turnover in the House will increase (and vice-versa), *ceteris paribus*. RGNP is the *real* GNP growth rate across each two-year election cycle. Because this measure represents the overall health of the economy, it is likely that incumbent legislators will be rewarded for their pereceived efforts in this regard, and be returned to political office. Therefore, we expect a negative relationship between RGNP and TURN. Finally, C-SPAN is a dummy variable equal to one for election cycles in which the C-SPAN cable television network provided significant/comprehensive coverage of U.S. House proceedings (1981-82 cycle and thereafter), and zero otherwise.[2] It is expected that, *ceteris paribus*, the presence of C-SPAN cameras will allow U.S. Representatives (incumbents) to use the institutional infrastructure of the U.S. House (one minute speeches, etc.) as an outlet for low-cost advertising. These parliamentary procedures are available to incumbent representatives only, and would be very expensive for potential challengers to replicate (i.e., to purchase in media markets), in either the party primaries or the general elections. It is, therefore, expected that TURN and CSPAN will be negatively related.

Two points regarding the model presented in equation (7.1) are worthy of note. First, it is recognized that the model presented above is quite parsimonious (see statistical models in previous chapters). This is important, because tests are to be conducted that decompose the means differences for turnover (i.e., the difference in turnover rates before and after C-SPAN), and these tests require interacting the C-SPAN dummy with all other regressors in the model, thus using valuable degrees of freedom within our data set (nobs=25). It is also necessary, however, that the model be specified correctly in order to perform these tests (Jackson and Lindley, 1989). Therefore, specification error tests will be carried out.

Second, the inclusion of the regressors in equation (7.1) is supported by research regarding the results of national elections that dates back at least to Kramer (1971) and Stigler (1973). Fair (1978) concisely synthesizes the debate among the alternative theories of Kramer and Stigler.[3] In part, Fair's work (1978: 161) interprets the theoretical disagreements in the literature concerning which variables to use in elections studies as measures of macroeconomic performance. The two most obvious economic variables to consider as possible measures of performance are (1) some measure of the rate of inflation, and (2) some measure of real output (Fair, 1978: 164). Therefore, the current study uses both INFL and RGNP, as suggested by Fair (1978, 1982 and 1996) and Mixon and Upadhyaya (1997).[4] These other works all employ relatively parsimonious empirical models to examine national election results in the United States.

Table 7.1 contains summary statistics for all of the variables used in our model, along with data sources. Although many scientific time series are stationary, quite often time series data are trending (Kennedy, 1998; Nelson and Plosser, 1982). Therefore, an Augmented Dickey-Fuller test (Dickey and Fuller, 1979) and a Phillips-Perron test (Phillips, 1987; Phillips and Perron, 1988) were performed on each macroeconomic time series. These results are reported in Table 7.2, and in each case, with the exception of INFL, these tests reject the null hypothesis of a unit root (suggesting that the series are stationary). In the case of INFL, stationarity is achieved upon

### Table 7.2 Unit Root Tests Results [*]

| | ADF | | PP | |
|---|---|---|---|---|
| *Variable* | *Level* | *First Difference* | *Level* | *First Difference* |
| TURN | -3.84** | n/a | -3.24** | n/a |
| QUIT | -4.01** | n/a | -3.99** | n/a |
| INFL | -2.74 | -3.80** | -2.75 | -7.76** |
| RGNP | -4.91*** | n/a | -7.31*** | n/a |

[*]    Notes: (1) ADF denotes the Augmented Dickey-Fuller test; (2) PP denotes the Phillips-Perron test; (3) ***[**] denotes the 0.01[0.05] significance level.

first-differencing the data series (Kennedy, 1998). For comparison, our regressions will employ both the level and first-difference form of INFL when this variable is included.

The results from seven versions of equation (7.1) above are presented in Table 7.3. The first version includes only QUIT and CSPAN as regressors, and is performed using Generalized Least Squares (GLS).[5] Here, both variables retain their expected signs and are significant. The

**Table 7.3 Summary of Regression Results dependent variable: TURN** [*]

| Regressors | (1) GLS | (2) OLS | (3) OLS | (4) GLS | (5) GLS | (6) GLS |
|---|---|---|---|---|---|---|
| constant | 5.09*** (2.39) | 8.80*** (2.65) | 8.72*** (2.53) | 4.74*** (2.26) | 4.87*** (2.18) | 4.13 (1.23) |
| QUIT | 1.27*** (6.25) | 1.14*** (3.30) | 1.12*** (3.06) | 1.44*** (5.29) | 1.29*** (4.98) | 1.33*** (4.47) |
| INFL | | | 0.02 (0.14) | -0.14 (-1.30) | | |
| ΔINFL | | | | | -0.04 (-0.30) | -0.03 (-0.19) |
| RGNP | | -0.30** (-2.01) | -0.30** (-1.86) | | | 0.07 (0.31) |
| CSPAN | -2.45*** (-2.11) | -3.61*** (-2.04) | -3.61** (-1.99) | -2.34*** (-2.10) | -2.54*** (-2.10) | -2.35* (-1.75) |
| F-statistic | 10.47*** | 7.00*** | 5.01*** | 8.54*** | 7.71*** | 5.87*** |
| Adj. R-sq. | 0.564 | 0.429 | 0.401 | 0.578 | 0.561 | 0.537 |
| RESET-F | 0.35 | 0.02 | 0.01 | 0.44 | 0.38 | 0.54 |
| BP-Q | 1.19 | 3.73 | 3.78 | 2.14 | 1.04 | 0.58 |
| LM-F | 0.55 | 2.31 | 2.27 | 1.19 | 0.47 | 0.28 |
| ARCH test | 1.09 | 0.09 | 0.06 | 0.02 | 0.96 | 0.61 |

[*]    Notes: BP-Q denotes the Box-Pierce Q-test. LM-F denotes the Lagrange Multiplier F-test. The numbers in parentheses above are $t$-values from significance tests for the regression parameters. ***(**)[*] denotes the 0.05(0.075)[0.10] level of significance.

parameter estimate for CSPAN suggests that turnover rates in the U.S. House are 2.5 percentage points lower in the C-SPAN era, *ceteris paribus*. This finding is consistent with the thesis of this chapter. Also, an additional percentage point in QUIT predictably leads to a 1.3 percentage point increase in TURN. Version (2) includes RGNP, which is negative and significant (at about the 0.06 level) as expected. Here, QUIT remains positive and insignificant, and CSPAN remains negative (though larger in absolute magnitude) and significant. This result suggests that House turnover rates are over 3.5 percentage points lower in the C-SPAN era, *ceteris paribus*. Also, three additional points added to RGNP predictably lead to a one percentage point decrease in House turnover rates. All of the results from the first two versions are striking, given that U.S. House turnover averaged about 16 percentage points from 1946-1994.

The remaining results mirror those of the first two versions of Table 7.3. Each equation estimated is jointly significant, and produces an adjusted R-square measure ranging from 0.401 to 0.578. Ramsey's RESET (Ramsey, 1969), a general test for various forms of specification error (e.g., omitted variables, errors in measurement, irrelevant variables, etc.), fails to reject the null hypothesis of "no specification error" in each case. This is important, given that decomposition tests, which are discussed below, rely upon proper specification. Also, none of the versions fail to reject the null hypotheses of "no serial correlation" and "no heteroscedasticity" with regard to the residuals.[6]

In each of the six models, the C-SPAN parameter is significant—usually at (approximately) the 0.05 level—and it ranges in magnitude from -2.34 to -3.61, suggesting that House turnover rates have been about 3 percentage points lower in the C-SPAN era (television era), *ceteris paribus*. Finally, both QUIT and RGNP are significant when included, but INFL and ΔINFL are not statistically significant in any version.

It is interesting to compare our estimates here with those regarding C-SPAN2's impact on Senate turnover from 1946-1998 (a similar time frame) presented in Mixon and Upadhyaya (2002). Table 7.4 compares summary data and estimates from the Mixon and Upadhyaya (2002) study on Senate turnover to those presented in this chapter. As the table points out, turnover in

### Table 7.4 Comparing the C-SPAN Network's Impact on U.S. House and Senate Turnover [*]

| Aspect | House Turnover | Senate Turnover |
| --- | --- | --- |
| Study | Ch. 7 of this book | Mixon and Upadhyaya (2002) |
| Time Frame | 1946-1994 | 1946-1998 |
| Mean Turnover Rates | 16.17 | 21.87 |
| Std. Dev. on Turnover | 5.12 | 12.81 |
| Coefficient of Variation on Turnover | 31.67% | 58.57% |
| C-SPAN(2) Parameter Estimates | -2.34 to -3.61 | -13.24 to -17.26 |
| Sig. Level of C-SPAN(2) Parameter Estimates | 0.10 to 0.05 | 0.05 to 0.01 |
| RGNP Parameter Estimates | 0.07 to -0.30 | -0.72 to -0.93 |
| Sig. Level of RGNP Parameter Estimates | >0.10 to 0.075 | >0.10 to 0.05 |

[*]    Sources: Mixon and Upadhyaya (2002) and the Authors.

the U.S. Senate was generally greater than that in the U.S. House over a similar time frame, although Senate turnover varied more widely than did House turnover. Both studies point out that turnover in each legislative branch was greater, *ceteris paribus*, in the post-television era. Again, however, the absolute difference is greater for the U.S. Senate (C-SPAN2) than the U.S. House (C-SPAN). In both cases, the pre- and post-television differences in turnover are statistically significant. Though interesting, a comparison of this sort leaves the analysis incomplete. More extensive tests are presented below that separate C-

SPAN's impact on turnover from other causal factors. These decomposition tests are also performed in Mixon and Upadhyaya (2002) for U.S. Senate turnover. After presenting decomposition tests for the House data, a better comparison can be made between the two studies.

## 7.4 Additional Statistical Exploration

As pointed out above, decomposing the means for the pre- and post-C-SPAN eras employs interaction terms, and thus consumes valuable degrees of freedom, given our relatively small sample size. As the RESET F-statistic suggests, version (2) of Table 7.3 provides an unbiased and parsimonious regression equation for use in a decomposition exercise (Jackson and Lindley, 1989). Interaction terms are used to more fully understand C-SPAN's role in reducing (increasing) House turnover (incumbent security). An approach that employs interactions is described by Jackson and Lindley (1989), and it is one that partitions the group means difference (i.e., the *total effect*) into components that measure the *structural effect* and the *residual effect*.[7] Beyond these, the subcomponents of the residual effect—the *constant effect* and the *coefficient effect*—are measured to provide a more accurate picture of the C-SPAN's importance.

The mean for TURN in the pre-C-SPAN era (i.e., 1946-1980) is 16.72, while its mean during the post-C-SPAN period (1982-1994) is 14.77. The total effect is the difference in these two means, or -1.95, and given the results in version (2) of Table 7.3 regarding the CSPAN parameter, U.S. House turnover is significantly lower in the C-SPAN era. That is, the total effect is significantly different from zero (at the 0.05 level; see Table 7.3). The structural effect indicates how House turnover would differ across the two eras under similar technological circumstances.[8] To calculate the structural effect, we obtained parameter estimates for the version (2) regression in Table 7.3, though using only the pre-C-SPAN era data (1946-1980). This, of course, necessitates omitting CSPAN on the right hand side of the equation. Once this equation is estimated, mean values for QUIT and RGNP from the post-C-SPAN era (1982-1994) are plugged into the equation, and a predicted value for TURN is obtained. In this case that value is 17.94, suggesting that the average value for TURN during the 1982-1994 period would have been 17.94 had C-SPAN cameras (or legislative television) not been present during that period. The structural effect is the post-C-SPAN era TURN prediction of 17.94 (assuming absence of cameras) minus the actual mean of TURN for the pre-C-SPAN era (16.72). Here, the structural effect is +1.22. Any differences across the two periods under similar technological circumstances (i.e., legislative television in both periods) is due to explanatory factors outside of the scope of our investigation. However, the remaining subcomponent of the total effect—the *residual effect*—is equal to the actual mean for TURN in the post-C-SPAN era (1982-1994) minus the post-C-SPAN era prediction for TURN (see above) of 17.94. In doing this calculation, tests suggest that the mean for TURN during 1982-1994 would have been 17.94 in the absence of C-SPAN. Instead, under the watchful eye of C-SPAN cameras, TURN averaged 14.77 during the 1982-1994 period. The difference, -3.17, represents the residual effect. The negative residual effect indicates that C-SPAN cameras worked to reduce House turnover by about 3.17 percentage points per election. This effect (-3.17) is significant at about the 0.12 level, based on an F-statistic of 2.211 (with 3, 20 degrees of freedom). This result, along with the previous computations, is presented in Table 7.5.

### Table 7.5 Decomposition Measures for C-SPAN's Impact on U.S. House Turnover [*]

| Total Effect | Structural Effect | Residual Effect | Constant Effect | Coefficient Effect |
|---|---|---|---|---|
| -1.95*** | 1.22 | -3.17* | -12.223** | 9.053 |
| (-2.04) | | [2.211] | (-1.50) | [1.115] |

[*]    Notes: [1] The numbers in parentheses above are *t*-statistics (one-tail test); those in brackets are F-statistics. [2] The *t*-statistic given for the total effect is taken from the TURN parameter estimate in version (2) of Table 7.3; the other *t*-statistic and F-statistics are computed as in Jackson and Lindley (1989). No statistical testing was performed for the estimate of the structural effect. [3] ***(**)[*] denotes the 0.05(0.075)[0.12] level of significance.

Because the residual effect alone can be an ambiguous measure in determining C-SPAN's role in reducing House turnover, its subcomponents are estimated (Jackson and Lindley, 1989). The first of these subcomponents is the *constant effect*, which measures the *direct* impact C-SPAN has had on turnover rates in the U.S. House. The constant effect is the estimated coefficient for CSPAN in version (2) of Table 7.3, with the addition of the two interaction terms (CSPAN•QUIT and CSPAN•RGNP). The constant effect is interpreted as the effect C-SPAN has on the intercept term of the U.S. House turnover function, and a significant finding *unambiguously* indicates that C-SPAN plays an important role in shaping U.S. House turnover rates (Jackson and Lindley, 1989). The constant effect has the predicted negative sign in this case, and its coefficient (-12.223) is significant at the 0.075 level (for a one-tail test), based on a *t*-value of -1.50. Lastly, the *coefficient effect* measures the *indirect* role C-SPAN has played regarding turnover. This indirect effect occurs through C-SPAN's interaction with QUIT and RGNP, and it is interpreted as the effect that C-SPAN has on the slope of the U.S. House turnover function. The coefficient effect, which is equal to the residual effect minus the constant effect, is *in*correctly signed (+9.053), although it is not significant, based on an F-statistic of 1.115 (with 2, 20 degrees of freedom). This result suggests that C-SPAN has not had a significant impact on U.S. House turnover rates through its interaction with QUIT and RGNP (both of these measures are also included in Table 7.5).

Once again, we are left with consideration and interpretation of our findings. Unlike in the previous chapters, the correctly signed and significant constant effect found here *unambiguously* supports the finding regarding the residual effect. As Jackson and Lindley (1989: 522) state, this is so "[r]egardless of the magnitude of the point estimate of the residual [effect]…" What is now left to do is compare these decomposition test results to those presented in Mixon and Upadhyaya (2002) regarding C-SPAN2's impact on U.S. Senate turnover rates. This is done in Table 7.6.

**Table 7.6 Comparing Decomposition Estimates of the C-SPAN Network's Impact on Turnover** *

| Aspect | House Turnover | Senate Turnover |
|---|---|---|
| Study | Ch. 7 of this book | Mixon and Upadhyaya (2002) |
| Time Frame | 1946-1994 | 1946-1998 |
| *Decomposition Measures:* | | |
| Total Effect | -1.95** | -14.555** |
| | (-2.04) | (-2.19) |
| Structural Effect | 1.22 | 1.325 |
| Residual Effect | -3.17# | -15.880*# |
| | [2.211] | [3.01] |
| Constant Effect | -12.223*# | -15.82*# |
| | (-1.50) | (-1.60) |
| Coefficient Effect | 9.053 | -0.06 |
| | [1.115] | [0.29] |

\*    Notes: The numbers above in parentheses are *t*-values (one-tail test); those in brackets are F-statistics. \*\*(\*#)[#] denote the 0.05(0.075)[0.12] level of significance.
Sources: Mixon and Upadhyaya (2002) and the Authors.

As Table 7.6 indicates, despite the large difference in the total and residual effects regarding the impact of legislative television on congressional turnover in the U.S House and U.S. Senate, the constant effects are remarkably similar (in both cases, the constant effects are statistically significant). This difference between the two is only 3.597 percentage points, and the two constant effects represent (in absolute value) about 73 and 76 percent of the mean values for TURN in the two studies, respectively (Mixon and Upadhyaya, 2002; the Authors). When the statistical estimates are decomposed, as in Jackson and Lindley (1989), it appears that the impact of C-SPAN and C-SPAN2 on U.S. House and U.S. Senate turnover rates, respectively, has been about the same across the two branches—legislative television has worked to reduce legislative turnover about 15 percentage points in each venue.

# 7.5 Concluding Thoughts

This chapter points out that there is a significant relationship between turnover rates in both the U.S. House (U.S. Senate) and the presence of C-SPAN (C-SPAN2) television cameras in the legislative body. Against a theoretical construct in which political services are modeled as search and/or experience goods, politicians often engage in persuasive advertising campaigns to win the votes of their constituents. Given the institutional infrastructure in the U.S. House (Senate), the presence of cameras on the legislative floor allows for political grandstanding and posturing on popular issues such as healthcare rights, anti-crime legislation, and educational finance plans (see Chapter 6) that would not likely take place otherwise (see Chapter 5). Such time is very costly for political challengers to replicate in the "marketplace of ideas." We provide evidence from various regression equations suggesting that turnover rates in the U.S. House (Senate) are significantly lower in the era of C-SPAN (C-SPAN2). The regression estimates are further supported by decomposition measures that separate the *individual* effect that C-SPAN plays from other structural effects in the macroeconomy or in the political arena. That such results can emanate from a process that has received so little attention in the economics literature is surprising. This chapter, at least partially, fills that void.

# Notes to Chapter 7

1. This proposition would need to account for the credibility problem that arises when one candidate provides information about his or her opponent (Crain and Goff, 1988: 12).

2. 1982 was the first year that C-SPAN provided full-time (or comprehensive) coverage (16 hours per day). Such lengthy coverage accommodates rising labor force participation rates, giving viewers the ability to watch outsite of daily work schedules.

3. Stigler's view suggests that a voter evaluates the current pronounce-ments and past performance of competing parties, forms an expecta-tion of his or her future utility under each party, and votes for the party that provides the maximum expected future utility. In this view, voters are well-informed and self-interested (Fair, 1978: 159). Kramer's model suggests that a voter supports the incumbent party if its *recent* performance has been satisfactory under some simple standard. In this view, information is costly and voters acquire only a small amount of information. The theory of voting behavior in the classic study by Downs (1957) is somewhere in between (Fair, 1978: 159-160).

4. For other recent approaches to elections modeling, see Alesina, Lon-dregan and Rosenthal (1996) and Barro (2002).

5. This study uses several tests to check for serial correlation and homoscedastic residuals (Gujurati, 1988; Kennedy, 1998; Greene, 2002). When detected, a GLS model is employed instead of OLS.

6. Given the macro-political economy models tested here, a check for heteroscadastic residuals was done, as suggested by Breusch and Pagan (1979) and Engle (1982).

7. As mentioned previously in Chapter 4, this partitioning or decom-position technique has proven helpful in labor market studies that examine racial or gender discrimination on wages using race or gender dummy variables. See Jackson and Lindley (1989) for a survey of this literature.

8. See Jackson and Lindley (1989) for a concise description of the decomposition technique and all of the relevant formulae and statisti-cal tests.

# Chapter 7 References

Alesina, A., J. Londregan and H. Rosenthal (1996) "The 1992, 1994 and 1996 elections: A comment and a forecast," *Public Choice* 88: 115-125.

Banaian, K. and W.A. Luksetich (1991) "Campaign spending in congressional elections," *Economic Inquiry* 29: 92-100.

Barro, R.J. (2002) *Nothing is sacred: Economic ideas for the new millennium*, Cambridge, MA: The MIT Press.

Breusch, T.S. and A.R. Pagan (1979) "A simple test for heteroscedasticity and random coefficient variation," *Econometrica* 47: 1,287-1,294.

Crain, W.M. and B.L. Goff (1988) *Televised legislatures: Political information technology ad public choice*, Boston, MA: Kluwer Academic Publishers.

cspan.org (2002), Internet web site for C-SPAN organization.

Dickey, D.A. and W.A. Fuller (1979) "Distribution of the estimators for autoregressive time series with a unit root," *Journal of the American Statistical Association* 74: 427-431.

Downs, A. (1957) *An economic theory of democracy*, New York, NY: Harper & Row.

*Economic Report of the President*, Council of Economic Advisors, Washington, D.C., various issues.

Engle, R.F. (1982) "Autoregressive conditional heteroscedasticity with estimates of the variance of United Kingdom inflation," *Econometrica* 50: 987-1,007.

Erikson, R.S. (1971) "The advantage of incumbency in congressional elections," *Polity* 3: 395-405.

Fair, R.C. (1978) "The effect of economic events on votes for president," *Review of Economics and Statistics* 60: 159-173.

Fair, R.C. (1982) "The effect of economic events on votes for president: 1980 results," *Review of Economics and Statistics* 64: 322-325.

Fair, R.C. (1996) "Econometrics and presidential elections," *Journal of Economic Perspectives* 10: 89-102.

Ferejohn, J.A. (1977) "On the decline of competition in congressional elections," *American Political Science Review* 71: 166-176.

Fiorina, M.P. (1977) "The case of vanishing marginals: The bureaucracy did it," *American Political Science Review* 71: 177-181.

Greene, W.H. (2000) *Econometric analysis*, Upper Saddle River, NJ: Prentice-Hall.

Gujurati, D.N. (1988) *Basic econometrics*, New York, NY: McGraw-Hill Book Company.

*Historical Statistics of the United States: Colonial Times to 1970* (1970), U.S. Department of Commerce, Bureau of the Census, Washington, D.C.

Jackson, J.D. and J.T. Lindley (1989) "Measuring the extent of wage discrimination: A statistical test and a caveat," *Applied Economics* 21: 515-540.

Kennedy, P. (1998) *A guide to econometrics*, Cambridge, MA: The MIT Press.

Kramer, G.H. (1971) "Short-term fluctuations in U.S. voting behavior, 1986-1964," *American Political Science Review* 65: 131-143.

Krehbiel, K. and J.R. Wright (1983) "The incumbency effect in congressional elections: A test of two explanations," *American Journal of Political Science* 27: 140-157.

Mayhew, D. (1974) "Congressional elections: The case of vanishing marginals," *Polity* 6: 295-317.

Mixon, F.G., Jr. and K.P. Upadhyaya (1997) "Gerrymandering and the *Voting Rights Act of 1982*: A public choice analysis of turnover in the U.S. House of Representatives," *Public Choice* 93: 357-371.

Mixon, F.G., Jr. and K.P. Upadhyaya (2002) "Legislative television as an institutional entry barrier: The impact of C-SPAN2 on Senate turnover, 1946-1998," *Public Choice* 112: 433-448.

Mueller, D.C. and T. Stratmann (1994) "Informative and persuasive campaigning," *Public Choice* 73: 319-333.

Nagler, J. and L. Leighley (1992) "Presidential campaign expenditures: Evidence on allocations and effects," *Public Choice* 73: 319-333.

Nelson, C.R. and C.I. Plosser (1982) "Trends and random walks in macroeconomic time series," *Journal of Monetary Economics* 10: 139-162.

Nelson, P. (1970) "Information and consumer behavior," *Journal of Political Economy* 77: 311-329.

Nelson, P. (1974) "Advertising as information," *Journal of Political Economy* 81: 729-754.

Ornstein, N.J., T.E. Mann and M.J. Malbin (1992) *Vital statistics on Congress 1991-1992*, Washington, D.C.: U.S. Congressional Quarterly, Inc..

Pearce, T. (1991) *Term limitation: The return to a citizen legislature*, Washington, D.C.: U.S. Term Limits Foundation.

Phillips, P.C.B. (1987) "Time series regression with unit roots," *Econometrica* 55: 277-301.

Phillips, P.C.B. and P. Perron (1988) "Testing for a unit root in time series regression," *Biometrica* 75: 335-346.

Ramsey, J.B. (1969) "Tests for specification errors in classical linear least-squares analysis," *Journal of the Royal Statistical Society* 31: 350-371.

*Statistical Abstract of the United States*, U.S. Department of Commerce, Bureau of the Census, Washington, D.C., various issues.

Stigler, G.J. (1961) "The economics of information," *Journal of Political Economy* 68: 213-225.

Stigler, G.J. (1973) "General economic conditions and national elections," *American Economic Review* 63: 160-167.

Will, G.F. (1992) *Restoration: Congress, term limits and the recovery of deliberative democracy*, New York, NY: The Free Press.

# 8

# *The Public Choice Approach to Legislative Television: New Avenues for Future Research*

*"Political audiences are much larger today than in earlier times, and the scrutiny of those audiences is more intense…Greater scrutiny may discourage honest candidates more than it does dishonest candidates…a society with commercialized fame, and thus intense media scrutiny, does not generate great leaders…it produces and attracts individuals who are adept at currying public favor and avoiding public blame." (Cowen, 2000: 51-54)*

## 8.1 Introduction

Although most extant literature about the impact of legislative television on representative democracy has been done by political journalists, the pioneering work of Crain and Goff (1986 and 1988) has brought this compelling subject into the mainstream of public choice research. To date, research on legislative television in the economics literature is largely represented by Crain and Goff (1986 and 1988), Greene (1991), Mixon, Hobson and Upadhyaya (2001), Mixon (2001 and 2002), Mixon and Upadhyaya (2002), and Mixon, Gibson and Upadhyaya (2003). As pointed out previously, most of these studies suggest that televising legislative sessions serves the political interests of expected utility maximizing legislators by acting as a barrier to entry into the legislative arena.

This chapter takes a brief look at possible additional avenues for the legislative television research agenda. In doing so, we will highlight some of the ongoing research in this field. We will also suggest some yet-to-be-explored fields in this area of public choice theory.

## 8.2 Legislative Television Research: Past, Present and Future

Though the Crain and Goff (1986 and 1988) series was extensive, their study left room for additional empirical verification of their central hypotheses. Tyrone, Mixon, Treviño and Minto (2003) undertake such an empirical verification by examining the political determinants of the earliest decision to adopt legislative television on a permanent basis at the national level in the United States. Data on legislator and district characteristics are used to explain the 1977 vote to adopt C-SPAN coverage of proceedings in the U.S. House of Representatives.

The Crain-Goff (1988) study built a conceptual framework for analyzing the 1986 vote to adopt C-SPAN2 television coverage of the U.S. Senate. That model utilizes 100 observations, yet it produces (potentially) much less information on the determinants of both "yea" and "nay" votes on legislative television adoption by federal legislators than the Tyrone et al. (2003) study promises to provide. Tyrone et al. (2003) gather data on the 386 votes in the U.S. House regarding C-SPAN adoption, and they employ a logit model (see Kennedy, 1998; Greene, 2000) to estimate the likelihood that any particular Representative voted "yea" on the legislative television bill (in 1977). This study employs many of the same regressors as Crain and Goff (1988), and finds that (1) the year in which a particular Representative was first elected to the U.S. House, (2) the absolute difference between a Representatives ACU score (American Conservative Union) for 1977 and the median ACU score for the U.S. House in 1977, and (3) the percent of each Congressional district's male labor force employed in white collar jobs are all significant determinants of a legislator's tendency to produce a "yea" vote on C-SPAN coverage in the U.S. House of Representatives. These findings support many of the Crain-Goff hypotheses. For instance, Crain and Goff (1988) suggest that some of the strongest opposition to legislative television comes from long-standing members of a legislature, who honed their political skills in a pre-television age. They also suggest that political ideological deviance (from the median legislator) lessens one's support for legislative television, given that the likelihood of using television to one's advantage becomes less as his or her political views become more extreme (in either direction). Lastly, white-collar employment measures the increased demand for information associated with higher education classes, and legislators facing such constituencies will respond by supporting television coverage, *ceteris paribus*. These hypotheses are captured, respectively, by the three regressors detailed above, and positive, negative and positive statistical estimates, respectively, for these three regressors supports these three Crain-Goff hypotheses (Tyrone et al., 2003).

Another recent study tests whether the political use of legislative television and campaign finance restrictions serve as complementary or substitutable forms of entry barriers (Mixon, Treviño and Minto, 2003). This study follows the main thrust of Crain and Goff (1988) by examining state-level characteristics (for 1976) regarding legislative television and campaign finance regulations, resulting in 50 observations.

Results from a simultaneous probit procedure (see Maddala, 1983) indicate that voter-constituent political activity or participation, as a form of pressure, is positively and significantly related to the stringency of a state's campaign finance regulations, as is the degree of representation in a state's lower legislative chamber (i.e., its house). The positive sign and significance of the presence of legislative television suggests that television coverage works to increase the restrictiveness of a state's campaign finance regulations. This last result for the first equation (in a two-equation system) supports the notion that legislative television and campaign finance restrictions serve incumbents as *complementary* institutional entry barriers.[1]

The individual topics of the Crain-Goff study, along with those of subsequent replications and extensions, are summarized in Table 8.1. The table indicates that there remain a few unexplored

### Table 8.1 Summary of the Focus and Sources of Prior Research on Legislative Television *

| Subject | Focus | Sources |
|---------|-------|---------|
| Adoption of Legislative Television | State Legislatures | |
| | U.S. House of Representatives | Mixon, 2001; Tyrone et al. 2003 |
| | U.S. Senate | Crain and Goff, 1988; Mixon, 2001 |
| Television and Legislative Output | State Legislatures | Crain and Goff, 1988 |
| | U.S. House of Representatives | |
| | U.S. Senate | |
| Television and Legislative Session Length | State Legislatures | Crain and Goff, 1988 |
| | U.S. House of Representatives | Mixon, Hobson and Upadhyaya, 2001 |
| | U.S. Senate | Mixon, Hobson, and Upadhyaya, 2001; MU-2003 |
| Television and use of Parliamentary Procedures | State Legislatures | |
| | U.S. House of Representatives | MU-2003 |
| | U.S. Senate | Mixon, 2002; Mixon, Gibson and Upadhyaya, 2003 |
| Television and Elections/ Legislative Turnover | State Legislatures | Crain and Goff, 1988; Greene, 1991 |
| | U.S. House of Representatives | Crain and Goff, 1988; MU-2003 |
| | U.S. Senate | Mixon and Upadhyaya, 2002 |

**Table 8.1 Summary of the Focus and Sources of Prior Research on Legislative Television (Continued)***

| Subject | Focus | Sources |
| --- | --- | --- |
| Legislative Television Compared to Other Political Entry Barriers | State Legislatures U.S. House of Representatives U.S. Senate | Mixon, Treviño and Minto, 2003 |

\* Note: "MU-2003" in the Sources column above refers to new evidence presented in this book (M=Mixon and U=Upadhyaya).

empirical avenues for testing some of the legislative television hypotheses presented in the economics literature. These include (1) examination of the legisalative television adoption decision in the 50 state legislative bodies, (2) examination of the impact of legislative television on congressional output in the U.S. House of Representatives and the U.S. Senate, (3) examination of the impact of legislative television on the use of various parliamentary procedures in the 50 state legislative bodies, and (4) a comparison of legislative television and other political entry barriers in the U.S. House of Representatives and the U.S. Senate.

The table also suggests that new theoretical and empirical investigations are now needed. A number of possibilities for future research effort are evident, such as:

- Empirical work similar to that presented in this volume but covering European and other legislatures and parliaments. This might offer further support for the Crain-Goff hypotheses.[2]

- Research concentrating on the American Executive Branch's response to increased media exposure accruing to the U.S. Congress from C-SPAN and C-SPAN2 coverage of legislative proceedings. As Crain and Goff (1988) and Mixon (2001) point out, one of the pressures for legislative branch adoption of television coverage was the skillful use of the media by the Executive branch over an extended time frame. Accordingly, television coverage of legislative sessions is one way Congress can compensate for the visibility advantage of the Presidency. Now, upon adoption of C-SPAN and C-SPAN2 in the Congress, the exposure pendulum has swung back toward the Congress. It might be interesting to investigate the possibility that U.S. Presidents have altered their use of televised press conferences, speeches, "town hall meetings," and other forms of communication since 1986, when both branches of the U.S. Congress were televised extensively.

- Scholarship examining the use of various procedures of the C-SPAN network by federal legislators to gain exposure. When possible, the network covers congressional press conferences, committee hearings, colloquia, panel discussions and other less formal means of communication and legislative activity. Given C-SPAN's commitment to gavel-to-gavel coverage of the legislature, its ability to cover ancillary events has been made easier by the creation of each successive offspring of the parent network (i.e., with the creation of C-SPAN2, then C-SPAN3, etc.). Some politicians are particularly adept at speaking informally to small groups of media or at managing committee hearings, which often pertain to high-profile issues. Exploration of the possibility that ancillary activity has changed since the creation and diffusion of C-SPAN's sub-units would be a useful extension of the literature on legislative television.

- A comparison of the use of filibustering and one minute speeches by younger legislators versus older legislators in the U.S. Congress might yield some interesting insights. Crain and Goff (1988) and Mixon (2001) point out that older legislators developed their political skills before television's impact became so large, and they will, therefore, use television less effectively than younger legislators, who have concentrated more heavily on using television to their political advantage. If so, it might be the case that younger legislators assumed a more active role in the one minute speeches (U.S. House) and filibuster (U.S. Senate) processes after the advent of C-SPAN (U.S. House) and C-SPAN2 (U.S. Senate) television coverage.

- Comparison of the electoral success rates for U.S. House/Senate seats by state legislators in states with legislative television versus those residing in states with little or no legislative television coverage might provide some insights into the value of media exposure in gaining support from voters and other constituents. This line of research would relate to the "television and elections/legislative turnover" research agenda highlighted in Table 8.1.

- Exploration of the impact of television on the conduct of judicial proceedings would seem to be an avenue worth exploring by public choice and law and economics scholars. Television coverage of judicial activity has become a prominent issue in the United States. Many legal scholars and national media critics and commentators have remarked that the excessive length of the O.J. Simpson trial was due in large part to the desire for media exposure on the part of the judges, witnesses, and litigators in the trial. Television coverage of the court hearings surrounding the 2000 Presidential election returns dispute in Florida also garnered large audiences. Conduct of judicial activity is likely to be influenced by the presence of television.

- Empirical investigation of the strategic use of language by legislators (e.g., use of irony, metaphor, humor, hints, indirectness, etc.) to sway colleagues and constituents toward one position or another, perhaps via the one minute speeches, Special Order Speeches, and filibustering segments of legislative business in the U.S. Congress (see Sally, 2002).

- Research on the periphery of this area of public choice might also yield some interesting findings. For instance, have the physical characteristics of federal legislators changed with the prominence of visual media? That is, do looks/appearance play a more prominent role in the success of politicians in the television age? Such an investigation would fit neatly within the "economics of beauty" research agenda already ongoing within the economics literature (Biddle and Hamermesh, 1994; Biddle and Hamermesh, 1998; Hamermesh, Meng, Zhang, 2002; Barro, 2002).

The list above is simply a beginning. There are certainly numerous other avenues for scholarly inquiry into this area of public choice economics.

## 8.3 Concluding Comments

The role and influence of legislative television in the political process is one of the most interesting, yet untapped, areas of public choice theory. This book has both summarized existing work and presented several new statistical findings regarding the importance and use of the media by elected officials. As this chapter suggests, there is much work left to be done. Hopefully, current and future generations of public choice scholars will endeavor to draw a more complete picture.

## Notes to Chapter 8

1. Details regarding both of these recent studies are available from the authors via e-mail (mixon@cba.usm.edu).

2. C-SPAN currently airs "Prime Ministers' Questions" from the British Parliament (tape-delayed) on Sunday evenings. It does not, however, cover daily activity from Parliament. Harry Grundy, a political scientist at the University of Cambridge (England), is currently exploring this avenue of research.

## Chapter 8 References

Barro, R. J. (2002) *Nothing is sacred: Economic ideas for the new millennium,* Cambridge, MA: The MIT Press.

Biddle, J.E. and D.S. Hamermesh (1994) "Beauty and the labor market," *American Economic Review* 84: 1,174-1,194.

Biddle, J.E. and D.S. Hamermesh (1998) "Beauty, productivity, and discrimination: Lawyers' looks and lucre," *Journal of Labor Economics* 16: 172-201.

Cowen, T. (2000) *What price fame?* Cambridge, MA: Harvard University Press.

Crain, W.M. and B.L. Goff (1986) "Televising legislatures: An economic analysis," *Journal of Law and Economics* 29: 405-421.

Crain, W.M. and B.L. Goff (1988) *Televised legislatures: Political information technology and public choice*, Boston, MA: Kluwer Academic Publishers.

Greene, K.V. (1991) "The nature of political services, legislative turnover, and television," *Public Choice* 70: 267-276.

Greene, W.H. (2000) *Econometric analysis*, Upper Saddle River, NJ: Prentice-Hall.

Hamermesh, D.S., X. Meng and J. Zhang (2002) "Dress for success—Does primping pay?" *Labour Economics* 9: 361-373.

Kennedy, P. (1998) *A guide to econometrics*, Cambridge, MA: The MIT Press.

Mixon, F.G., Jr. (2001) "A discrete-time hazard model of the adoption of legislative television: Evidence from the U.S. Congress, 1961-1986," *Applied Economics* 33: 1,881-1,887.

Mixon, F.G., Jr. (2002) "Does legislative television alter the relationship between voters and politicians?" *Rationality and Society* 14: 109-128.

Mixon, F.G., Jr., M.T. Gibson and K.P. Upadhyaya (2003) "Has legislative television changed legislator behavior? C-SPAN2 and the frequency of Senate filibustering," *Public Choice*, forthcoming.

Mixon, F.G., Jr., D.L. Hobson and K.P. Upadhyaya (2001) "Gavel-to-gavel congressional television coverage as political advertising: The impact of C-SPAN on legislative sessions," *Economic Inquiry* 39: 351-364.

Mixon, F.G., Jr., L.J. Treviño and T.C. Minto (2003) "Are legislative t.v. and campaign finance regulations complementary entry barriers? Evidence from the states," Unpublished Manuscript.

Mixon, F.G., Jr. and K.P. Upadhyaya (2002) "Legislative television as an institutional entry barrier: The impact of C-SPAN2 on turnover in the U.S. Senate, 1946-1998," *Public Choice* 112: 433-448.

Sally, D. (2002) "'What an ugly baby!' Risk dominance, sympathy, and the coordination of meaning," *Rationality and Society* 14: 78-108.

Tyrone, M.J., F.G. Mixon, Jr., L.J. Treviño and T.C. Minto (2003) "Politics and the adoption of legislative television: An analysis of the U.S. House vote on C-SPAN," *European Journal of Law and Economics*, forthcoming.

# Legislative Television Reading List

The legislative television reading list that appears below is not a comprehensive list. We sought to narrow our list to articles appearing in the economics literature during (approximately) the past two decades. Even with this restriction, we are sure to have omitted something. The first two entries in our list, however, are certain to be the seminal pieces in any good list of readings on legislative television. They build a good foundation for future exploration in this area.

*Reading List:*

Crain, W.M. and B.L. Goff (1986) "Televising legislatures: An economic analysis," *Journal of Law and Economics* 29: 405-421.

Crain, W.M. and B.L. Goff (1988) *Televised legislatures: Political information technology and public choice*, Boston, MA: Kluwer Academic Publishers.

Greene, K.V. (1991) "The nature of political services, legislative turnover, and television," *Public Choice* 70: 267-276.

Mixon, F.G., Jr. (2001) "A discrete-time hazard model of the adoption of legislative television: Evidence from the U.S. Congress, 1961-1986," *Applied Economics* 33: 1,881-1,887.

Mixon, F.G., Jr. (2002) "Does legislative television alter the relationship between voters and politicians?" *Rationality and Society* 14: 109-128.

Mixon, F.G., Jr., M.T. Gibson and K.P. Upadhyaya (2003) "Has legislative television changed legislator behavior? C-SPAN2 and the frequency of Senate filibustering," *Public Choice*, forthcoming.

Mixon, F.G., Jr., D.L. Hobson and K.P. Upadhyaya (2001) "Gavel-to-gavel congressional television coverage as political advertising: The impact of C-SPAN on legislative sessions," *Economic Inquiry* 39: 351-364.

Mixon, F.G., Jr., L.J. Treviño and T.C. Minto (2003) "Are legislative t.v. and campaign finance regulations complementary entry barriers? Evidence from the states," Unpublished Manuscript.

Mixon, F.G., Jr. and K.P. Upadhyaya (2002) "Legislative television as an institutional entry barrier: The impact of C-SPAN2 on turnover in the U.S. Senate, 1946-1998," *Public Choice* 112: 433-448.

Tyrone, M.J., F.G. Mixon, Jr., L.J. Treviño and T.C. Minto (2003) "Politics and the adoption of legislative television: An analysis of the U.S. House vote on C-SPAN," *European Journal of Law and Economics*, forthcoming.

# The Authors

**Franklin G. Mixon, Jr.** is a Business Advisory Council Professor of Economics at The University of Southern Mississippi. He received his PhD in economics from Auburn University in 1992, and has also held a faculty post at Southeastern Louisiana University. His research generally follows the public choice tradition, and his recent work has been published in the *Journal of Money, Credit, and Banking*, *Economic Inquiry*, *Southern Economic Journal*, *Public Choice*, *Rationality and Society*, *Economics of Governance*, and *Public Finance Review*. He is currently serving on the editorial boards of the *International Journal of Business and Economics* and the *Journal of Economics and Finance Education*.

**Kamal P. Upadhyaya** is an Associate Professor of Economics at the University of New Haven. He received his PhD in economics from Auburn University in 1993, and he has also held faculty posts at Salisbury State University and Pennsylvania State University. His research examines international trade, macroeconomics and economic development, and it has recently been published by *Economic Inquiry*, *Economics Letters*, *Journal of Development Studies*, *Applied Economics*, *International Trade Journal*, *Public Choice*, and *Journal of Public Finance and Public Choice*. Recently, he co-authored a book (with Mixon) on national saving titled *The Political Economy of National Saving in the U.S.: Evidence on the Social Opportunity Costs of Public Policy* (Writers Club Press, 2002).

0-595-27086-7

www.ingramcontent.com/pod-product-compliance
Lightning Source LLC
Chambersburg PA
CBHW020257290526
45784CB00003B/1276